October 6, 2002

Saint Josemaría Escrivá

Michele Dolz

This is a limited edition biography
issued on the occasion of the
canonization of Josemaría Escrivá.

First edition: October 2002

Imprimatur: + Javier Echevarría, Prelate of Opus Dei
Prelatic Curia, June 26, 2002

Editorial coordinator: *Francesc Castells*
Graphic design: *MCM, Marketing Communication Mix, Firenze*
Photos: *Historical Archives of the Opus Dei Prelature, Scala Archives*

"How precious is your kindness, O God! The children of men take refuge in the shadow of your wings. . . For with you is the fountain of life, and in your light we see light." (Ps. 36(35):8, 10). The Blessed Trinity granted its light to Saint Josemaría so that he could contemplate deeply the mystery of Jesus Christ, *the light of the human race* (cf. Jn 1:4), affording him a very profound insight into the mystery of the Incarnate Word and making him understand that human realities become the setting and means of sanctification in the heart of a person born again in Christ.

On October 6, Pope John Paul II will canonize the founder of Opus Dei. I ask the Lord that this date may entail for everyone a new summons to conversion, to let the Holy Spirit sanctify us, so that our hearts may love God and our neighbor ever more and more.

In this book, the author highlights features of the new saint and offers us some of his teachings. Saint Josemaría Escrivá invites us to follow, right where we are, the path of Christ, who *did and taught* (cf. Acts 1:1), uniting example and speech. The life of Saint Josemaría is an invitation to put into practice his message: to seek, to find, and to love Christ amid our family, professional, and social duties. His life summons us to charity, to love, with a panorama as old and as new as the Gospel.

In union with the Holy Father, we will never tire of the realization that the spirit of Christ should inform every corner of our existence, as John Paul II said on the occasion of the Rome celebration of the centennial of the birth of the founder of Opus Dei.

I desire that, at the canonization of Josemaría Escrivá, and through the sovereign intercession of our Lady, in communion with the entire Church, the Holy Spirit may fill us with the peace and the joy of the children of God in Christ Jesus.

+ Javier Echevarría
Prelate of Opus Dei

CONTENTS

Works

Chronology

The Life of Josemaría Escrivá

Life

It is impossible to do justice to the life of a saint in a few pages; perhaps not even in several volumes. External facts can be described, but who can plumb the depths of a holy life? The saint is a man of God, a soul identified with Jesus Christ, "as you, Father, are in me and I in you" (*Jn* 17, 21). This is the sense we get when we approach the life of Saint Josemaría Escrivá, as we now attempt to do.

But saints aren't supermen, nor persons out of the ordinary, beings impossible to capture in words. It is precisely to Saint Josemaría that we owe a fundamental teaching in this regard: "Let's not deceive ourselves: in our life we will find vigor and victory and depression and defeat. This has always been true of the earthly pilgrimage of Christians, even of those we venerate on the altars. Don't you remember Peter, Augustine, Francis? I have never liked biographies of saints which naively—but also with a lack of sound doctrine—present their deeds as if they had been confirmed in grace from birth. No. The true life stories of Christian heroes resemble our own experience: they fought and won; they fought and lost. And then, repentant, they returned to the fray."

The struggle to identify oneself with Christ, however, is a difficult, sincere, joyful, and persevering endeavor. But, above all, it is a work of the Holy Spirit, the Spirit of Love, which makes us into children of God in his Son.

A CHRISTIAN FAMILY

Little Josemaría was only two years old when he got sick, so seriously sick that the doctor expected him to die. Around him, the Escrivá household fell silent. Finally, Doctor Campos, who had done everything possible to save him, told his father:

"He won't last through the night."

The parents of Saint Josemaría, Jose Escrivá (1867–1924) and Dolores Albas (1877–1941).

But José Escrivá and his wife Dolores Albás Escrivá were devout Catholics who prayed to God with great faith for their child's cure. Dolores promised the Blessed Mother that, if he got well, she would bring him on pilgrimage to the ancient chapel of Torreciudad perched on a bluff in the foothills of the Pyrenees.

The next morning the doctor returned to call on the family. "At what time did the little boy die?" he asked. The boy's father, unable to contain his joy, replied, "Not only didn't he die, but he seems completely recovered!"

Josemaría was born in Barbastro, a small town in upper Aragon, on January 9, 1902. His father, well known in town, was a young textile merchant with strong Christian principles. His mother was entirely devoted to her family and to raising their two children, Carmen and Josemaría. Later, others would arrive: Asunción (nicknamed Chon), Lolita, Rosario, and years later, Santiago.

On the right, the chapel of our Lady of Torreciudad.

"I remember those happy days of my childhood," Josemaría reminisced: "My mother, my father, my sisters and I always went together to Mass. My father gave us the alms that we brought to the disabled man who leaned against the wall of the bishop's residence. After that, I would run ahead to get holy water to give to my family.[1] Then, Holy Mass. Afterwards, every Sunday, in the chapel of the Christ of the Miracles, we prayed the Creed." At home, he said prayers that he would never forget: "Even now, I recite every morning and evening the

prayers that my mother taught me. . . . When I was
six or seven my mother brought me to her confessor,
and I was glad to go." A little later, on April 23,
1912, he made his First Holy Communion on the
feast of St. George, as was the custom in that part of
Spain.

José dedicated a good deal of time to his
children. Young Josemaría used to wait impatiently
for him to come home and greeted him by putting
his hands in his father's pockets, hoping to find
some candy. In winter the father would take his son
for a walk, stopping to buy roasted chestnuts from
street vendors so Josemaría could amuse himself by
warming his hands with them in the pockets of his
father's overcoat.

Dolores was calm but hard-working. "I don't
ever remember having seen her with nothing to do.
She was always busy, whether knitting, sewing or
mending some piece of clothing, reading . . . I never
remember seeing her idle."

And she was not an unusual person; she was
just like everyone else, friendly, a good mother of a
Christian family.

"When I was a child, two things really bothered
me: having to kiss my mother's friends when they
came to visit, and wearing new clothes. When I was
dressed up in new clothes, I would hide under the
bed and stubbornly refuse to come out. My mother
would give a few gentle taps on the floor, with one
of the canes my father used, and then I would come
out—for fear of the cane, not for any other reason.

"Then my mother would say to me affectionately, 'Josemaría, be ashamed only of sin.' Many years later it dawned on me what a depth of meaning lay in those words."

So life continued in that household. But soon sorrows arrived. In 1910 Rosario died, only 9 months old. Two years later, Lolita died at the age of 5. A year later, Chon died at the age of 8. Troubled by all this misfortune, Josemaría told his mother, not realizing the pain it would cause her,

"Next year it's my turn."
"Don't worry," she consoled him, "I offered you to our Lady, and she will take care of you."

The birthplace of Josemaría Escrivá.

Around the same time the career of José Escrivá suffered an abrupt turn due to the unjust actions of one of his partners. The family's savings were lost, although the parents attempted to keep this from the children. Years later Josemaría found a supernatural explanation for these painful events. "I have always made those I had around me suffer a lot. I didn't provoke catastrophes. But our Lord, to hit me, who was the nail—(pardon me, Lord), landed one blow on the nail and a hundred on the horseshoe. I saw my father as the personification of Job. He lost three daughters, one after the other in consecutive years, and then lost his fortune.

"And life went on. My father reacted with heroism, after becoming sick, as I now realize, from undergoing such great misfortunes and worries. He was left with two children and my mother. And he found the strength to bring us forward, not sparing himself any humiliation to provide us with a decent life. He might have remained in a position that was very comfortable for those times, if he had not been a Christian and a gentleman, as they say in my country. I can't remember a harsh gesture from him. I recall him as always calm, with a cheerful look. He died worn out, when he was only 57. He died exhausted, but he was always smiling."

Saint Josemaría must certainly have recalled his own family's experience when, teaching the spirit of Opus Dei, he encouraged Christian parents to make their own homes into bright and cheerful ones. Matrimony, he said, is "a divine pathway, a vocation, and this has many consequences for personal holiness and for apostolate." The first and principal field of sanctification and apostolate is precisely the family. "Christian couples should be aware that they are called to sanctify themselves and to sanctify others, that they are called to be apostles and that their first apostolate is in their home. They should understand that founding a family, educating their children, and exercising a Christian influence in society, is a supernatural task. The effectiveness and the success of their life—their happiness—depend to a great extent on their awareness of their specific mission

The baptismal font of the Cathedral of Barbastro, where Josemaría was baptized on January 13, 1902. It is now in Rome, in the Prelatic Church of Our Lady of Peace.

1. He is referring here to the custom of dipping one's hand in the holy water and then passing it along to friends or relatives who follow behind by dabbing their fingers with it.

The family

"Husband and wife are called to sanctify their married life and to sanctify themselves in it. . . . Family life, the marriage union, the care and education of children, the effort to provide for the needs of the family as well as for its security and development, the relationships with other persons who make up the community, all these are among the ordinary human situations that Christian couples are called upon to sanctify" (Christ Is Passing By, 23).

FOOTPRINTS IN THE SNOW

On Wednesday, January 9, 1918, Josemaría turned sixteen. The city of Logroño lay peaceful under a heavy snowfall. The temperature hovered around zero degrees Fahrenheit. No one went out unless they absolutely had to.

José had found work in Logroño as a sales clerk in a business similar to the one of which he had previously been proprietor. So the family had moved there. Leaving Barbastro had not been easy for any of them, including Josemaría, now a budding teenager.

With his brother and sister, Santiago and Carmen.

On one of those wintry days the young man looked down at the snow and saw footprints left by bare feet. He realized that they had been made by one of the Carmelite friars newly arrived in the city. He wondered: If others can make such sacrifices for God, can't I offer him something? It was a thought destined to stick with him for the rest of his life.

"Our Lord was preparing me in spite of myself, using apparently innocuous things to instill a divine restlessness in my soul. Thus I came to understand very well the love, so human and so divine, that moved Saint Thérèse of the Child Jesus when, leafing through the pages of a book, she suddenly came upon a picture of one of the Redeemer's wounded hands. Things like that happened to me too—things that moved me and led me to daily Communion, to purification, to confession, and to penance.

"I began to have intimations of Love, to realize that my heart was asking for something great, and that it was love . . . I didn't know what God wanted of me, but it was evident that I had been chosen for something."

What could he do? Pray, certainly. Ask the Lord to enlighten his heart. He began to use the words of the blind man of the Gospel as an aspiration: *Domine, ut videam!*—Lord make me see what you want from me. And his life followed the course of a normal high school student. He was a good student, got excellent grades, and dreamed of being an architect.

If only he knew what his calling was. In any

case, he answered "yes," a yes to whatever it was that God had called him to. He thought that he would be better prepared for his vocation if he became a priest. "One fine day I told my father that I wanted to be a priest; it was the only time I saw him cry. He had other plans in mind, but he did not object. He told me, 'My son, think it over carefully. A priest has to be a saint. . . . It is very hard not to have a home, a love on earth. Think about it a bit more, but I will not oppose your decision.'"

He advised Josemaría to speak with a priest he knew. This priest spoke with the youth and assured his father that his son had a vocation to the priesthood. He still had to finish high school. Now that he had ruled out studying architecture, his father advised him to pursue a degree in law and to make these civil studies compatible with his commitments in the seminary. God used the example of his father to introduce into Josemaría's heart a conviction that he passed on throughout his life: "It is no 'sacrifice' for parents when God asks them for their children. Neither, for those that he calls, is it a sacrifice to follow him. Rather it is an immense honor, a motive for a great and holy pride, a mark of predilection, a very special affection that God has shown at a particular time, but that he has foreseen from all eternity."

Alter Christus, ipse Christus

"To follow Christ—that is the secret. We must accompany him so closely that we come to live with him, like the first Twelve did; so closely, that we become identified with him. Soon we will be able to say, provided we haven't put obstacles in the way of grace, that we have put on, have clothed ourselves with our Lord Jesus Christ" (Friends of God, *299*).

THE SEMINARY YEARS

"Time passed, and many hard and distressing things happened, which I will not tell you about. Although they do not make me suffer, you would be saddened by them. They were axe blows struck at the tree by God our Lord. From that tree, he was shaping a beam that would be used, in spite of its weakness, to do his Work. Almost without realizing it, I kept repeating *Domine, ut videam! Domine, ut sit!* [Lord, let me see! Lord, let it be!] I did not know what it was he wanted, but I went forward . . . without doing anything unusual, working with just average intensity . . . Those were the years in Saragossa."

He arrived at the Seminary of San Carlos in Saragossa in 1920, after having completed the first year at the diocesan seminary in Logroño as a day student. At San Carlos, because of his comportment and human qualities, he was named a prefect by Cardinal Soldevila, who shortly afterwards was assassinated by anti-religious fanatics.

He went every day to the nearby basilica where Our Lady of the Pillar is venerated in accord with an ancient tradition. He entrusted himself to her while waiting for a definitive answer regarding the will of God. "And I, half-blind, was always waiting for the answer. Why am I becoming a priest? Our Lord wants something: what is it? And in Latin—not very elegant Latin— . . . I kept repeating *Domine, ut videam! Ut sit! Ut sit!* What is it that you want and that I don't know?"

St. Josemaría as a seminarian. By his side, his uncle Carlos Albas.

Here his piety welled up in tender child-like gestures. He recounted, for example, "I was able to stay in the Church one day after the doors were locked. With the complicity of one of the good priests . . . I climbed the few steps so well known to those who escort the little children, and getting up close, I kissed the image of our Mother." "I knew that this was not customary; that kissing her cloak was reserved exclusively for children and authorities. . . . However, I was and am sure that my Mother of the Pillar was pleased that I disregarded the protocol on that one occasion."

His prayer to Mary was accompanied by prolonged adoration of the Eucharist. He spent much time in the chapel of the seminary, at times praying for an entire night from an upper balcony that had a view of the Tabernacle.

In November, 1924, an urgent call came from Logroño: his father had died unexpectedly. "My father died exhausted, but still with a smile on his lips. . . ." In addition to their sorrow, the Escrivá's were now in an even tighter spot economically than before. Still in mourning, he was ordained a priest in the chapel of the seminary on March 28, 1925. He celebrated his first Mass in the Basilica of Our Lady of the Pillar, at the feet of the beloved Madonna he had prayed to

The Basilica of our Lady of the Pillar, where he celebrated his first Mass.

so often. His mother, his sister, and a few close friends were present, and the Mass was said for the repose of the soul of his father.

From that moment on, Holy Mass became even more central in his life. Within the Mass he received some of the most important inspirations from God. Upon the altar he deposited his requests, from there he always drew his strength. Conveying his own experience, he counseled: "Keep struggling, so that the Holy Sacrifice of the Altar really becomes the center and the root of your interior life, and so your whole day will turn into an act of worship—an extension of the Mass you have attended and a preparation for the next. Your whole day will then be an act of worship that overflows in aspirations, visits to the Blessed Sacrament and the offering up of your professional work and your family life."

AMONG THE POOR AND THE SICK

"What would you like to do if you were rich, very rich?"

This unusual question came from the lips of young Father Josemaría, fresh from his priestly ordination and caught up in his first assignment to Perdiguera, a village of some 800 souls not far from Saragossa. He was speaking with the son of the family with whom he lodged, a little boy who spent each day pasturing goats, and to whom he taught catechism each evening in preparation for First Holy Communion. "One day, to see how much he was learning, it occurred to me to ask him:

'What would you like to do if you were rich, very rich?' 'What does being rich mean?' he answered. 'To be rich is to have a lot of money, to have a bank . . .' 'And . . . what is a bank?'

"I explained it in a simple way and continued: 'To be rich is to have a lot of land, and instead of goats, very big cows. And to go to meetings, change suits three times a day . . . What would you do if you were rich?' His eyes opened wide, and then at last he said: 'I'd eat lots of bowls of soup with wine in it!'

"All our ambitions come down to that; nothing is worthwhile. Strangely enough I have never forgotten that story. It struck me and made me think: 'Josemaría, it is the Holy Spirit speaking.' God in his wisdom did this to teach me that the things of the earth, all of them, come to that: very, very little."

In Perdiguera, the house where Josemaría Escrivá lived.

He had arrived in Perdiguera three days after his ordination, sent to substitute for a priest on an emergency basis. It was an out-of-the-way village in a then-underdeveloped region. The first thing he had to do upon arrival was clean the church. The second thing he did was to reorganize the celebration of worship. He introduced a sung Mass, Benediction of the Blessed Sacrament, confessions, catechism . . . Ignorance and neglect reigned. In a short time the spiritual climate changed, to the point that fifty years later, at the time of his death,

"Domina ut sit!"
*is the aspiration
carved by
Josemaría in
the base of the
statue of our
Lady of the Pillar,
May 24, 1924.*

the people still fondly remembered Father Josemaría's short stay.

Nevertheless the young priest was aware that God was calling him to another task that he did not yet know, and once his duties of filling in for the parish priest were through, he was back in Saragossa with the idea of finishing his law degree. This he did, and with his usual good grades. With the permission of the archbishop he transferred to Madrid to pursue his doctorate in law, which at that time could only be obtained at the Spanish capital's Central University. He suspected that he would be able to carry out whatever God had in store for him more easily there.

In Madrid he immediately encountered the misery of the poor inhabitants of shantytowns, which housed mainly newcomers from the countryside for whom the promise of jobs in industry had been a mirage. He took up lodging in a modest residence for priests on Larra Street sponsored by the Congregation of Apostolic Ladies of the Sacred Heart of Jesus. These women took care of the Foundation for the Sick and many other charitable works: catechism in areas without schools, food pantries for the indigent, night classes, dispensaries. Father Josemaría immediately made himself available to help in these services to the marginalized and pitched in to help these pious women while he attended to his studies.

From 1927 to 1931 he was chaplain of the Foundation for the Sick, dedicated to assisting people who, in addition to being abandoned, were easy targets for anti-Catholic ideologies and often hostile toward the clergy. Many years later, on a return visit to that part of Madrid, now completely changed, he recalled, "When I was 25, I used to come frequently to these undeveloped areas to wipe away tears, to help whoever was in need, to bring a little warmth to the children, the old people, and the sick; and to receive a lot of love in return and . . . once in a while, a pelting with rocks."

He walked from one part of the city to another bringing the sacraments to the sick and dying according to information provided by the Apostolic Ladies. Other times he went to hear the confessions of children. He recalls having prepared thousands for their First Holy Communion in this era. There was no lack of dramatic and tense personal situations that he soothed with charity and doctrine.

He rightly intuited that God's plan for him did not lay in this expansive work of charity. Nonetheless, he threw himself into it heart and soul, especially after receiving his founding vision on October 2, 1928. Among the poor, the sick, children—here was where he sought the strength needed to set in motion the immense project that God had placed on his shoulders that day. It was a school of suffering where his soul would be tempered to his mission.

As he would later teach his spiritual sons who were called to holy orders, they had to be priests one-hundred-percent, priestly priests, priests at the service of souls. "To serve is the greatest joy that a soul can experience, and this is what we priests must do. Day and night at the service of all—otherwise, we are not priests. A priest should love the young and the old, the poor and the rich, the sick and the children. He should prepare himself well to celebrate Mass. He should welcome and take care of souls one by one, like a shepherd who knows his flock and calls each sheep by name. We priests do not have rights. I like to think of myself as a servant of all, and in this title I take pride."

While he gave himself to that tireless ministry of charity, his soul seemed to glimpse the approach of light from God. Seized with an overflowing zeal, he shouted or at times sang out the aspiration spoken by Jesus himself: *Ignem veni mittere in terram, et quid volo nisi ut accendatur?* ("I have come to cast fire on the earth; what will I but that it be kindled!").

King's Hospital, where Father Josemaría cared for the terminally ill.

THE FOUNDING OF OPUS DEI

It was October 2, 1928, the feast of the Guardian Angels. Father Josemaría would never forget the sound of the church bells . . .

He was making a retreat during these first few days of October. A little less than a year earlier his family had moved to Madrid. They were living in a small apartment supported only by whatever he could earn. Without neglecting his ministry among the poor and sick, Father Josemaría tutored private students and taught courses in Canon Law and Roman Law at the Cicuéndez Academy. On top of that, he continued working towards his doctorate in law. That week, after his September examinations, seemed an opportune moment to make the retreat being offered for diocesan clergy in the central house of the Vincentians.

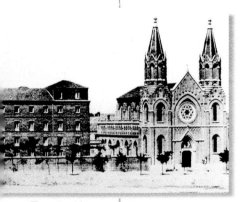

The retreat house of the Vincentian Fathers. Here, on October 2, 1928, Opus Dei was born.

On October 2, after Mass, Fr. Josemaría returned to his room and began to put his notes in order: resolutions and inspirations taken down during his prayer, and meditated upon many times already. There, suddenly, he saw the long-awaited will of God. He always used the verb *to see* on the rare occasions in which he referred to that supernatural intervention: it was an intellectual vision of Opus Dei such as God wished it to be and as it would be down through the centuries.

What did he see? In an ineffable way, he saw people of every nation and race, of every age and culture, seeking and finding God right in the middle of their ordinary life, their work, their family, their friendships. People who looked for Jesus in order to love him and to live his holy life until they were completely transformed and made into saints. Saints in the world. A tailor saint, a baker saint, an office saint, a factory worker saint. A saint, seemingly like everyone else around him, but deeply identified with Jesus Christ. A person who directs all his activity to God, who sanctifies his work, who sanctifies himself in his work and sanctifies others through it. A person who Christianizes his surroundings, who with warm simple friendships also helps his neighbor to come closer to Jesus—someone whose Christian faith is contagious.

It was an overwhelming vision, a vision of the baptismal vocation lived to the full. Ordinary Christians, the laity, becoming apostles, who speak of God with naturalness, who raise Christ to the peak of every human activity. Everyday people who assume in all its depth a participation in the priesthood of Christ by offering the sanctifying sacrifice of their own lives, whole and entire, every day.

He envisioned a way of holiness and apostolate to serve the Church, for all of this was the Church and nothing but the Church. The will of God was clear: open up to persons of any age, civil status, and social condition a new possibility of vocation for the Church right in the middle of the street. It was a vision of the Church that promised to bear abundant fruit of holiness and apostolate the whole world over. This would come about because Christians in the world would be able to renew the world without separating themselves from it in the least.

Father Josemaría fell to his knees, deeply moved. The bells from the Church of Our Lady of the Angels chimed, celebrating the feast of the Guardian Angels. "I was 26, had God's grace and good humor and nothing else. And I had to do Opus Dei," he recalled.

Prudence led him to inquire whether something like this might already exist in the Church. He contacted Church entities throughout Europe, from Spain to Poland, eventually realizing the originality of the message he had received. God was asking him for something specific and new. He therefore began to gather together persons—students, professionals, priests—to whom he could transmit this ideal. One of them remembers him as an inspired priest who had decided to devote his whole life to the fulfillment of that plan.

"But do you think this is possible?" he asked. To which Father Josemaría answered: "Look, this isn't something I've thought up; it's from God."

He requested prayers from everyone he knew, because he realized the huge gap between what God wanted and what he personally was capable of. The only solution was to become very holy. And this he desired with all his soul. On one occasion, one of the Apostolic Ladies was dying. The chaplain went to visit her and later wrote in his personal diary:

One of the bells of the parish of our Lady of the Angels.

"Without my having thought of this ahead of time, it occurred to me to ask her, and I did ask her, 'Mercedes, ask our Lord, from heaven, that if I am not going to be a priest who is not just good, but holy, that he take me young, as soon as possible.' Later I made the same request to two lay persons, a young lady and a boy, and every day, at Communion, they make this prayer for me to the good Jesus."

At the beginning he thought he should spread this ideal only among men. It was the normal thing that Catholic institutions be either male or female. But God always has the last word. On February 14, 1930, while celebrating Mass, he saw further what God wanted from him. God wished the Work to develop its apostolate among women as well. The consequences of the activities of the women would be immeasurable, because, as the founder put it, "Women are called to bring to the family, society and the Church characteristics which are their own and which they alone can give: their gentle warmth and untiring generosity, their love for detail, their quick-wittedness and intuition, their simple and deep piety, their constancy." Their role is to bring God into the world precisely through their femininity.

Father Josemaría continued to dream, convinced as he was that the will of God would be fulfilled. Ordinary Christians were to bring Christ into the very heart of the world. God in turn confirmed this supernatural hope by introducing himself again and again into his soul. One such visitation occurred on August 7, 1931. Saint Josemaría was celebrating Mass. "I think I then renewed my resolve to dedicate my entire life to the fulfillment of God's will: the Work of God. (A resolve that, right now, I again renew with all my soul.) The time for the Consecration arrived. At the very moment when I elevated the Sacred Host, without losing the necessary recollection, without becoming distracted (for I had just made mentally, the Offering to the Merciful Love), there came to my mind, with extraordinary force and clarity, that

St. Josemaría with Juan Jimenez Vargas and Ricardo Fernandez Vallespin, two of the first faithful of Opus Dei.

passage of Scripture, *Et ego, si exaltatus fuero a terra, omnia traham ad me ipsum* ("And I, if I be lifted up from the earth, will draw all things unto me"[*Jn* 12:32]). (Ordinarily, before the supernatural, I feel afraid. Later comes the 'Do not be afraid, it is I.') And I understood that there will be men and women of God who will lift the cross, with the teachings of Christ, to the pinnacle of all human activities. . . . And I saw our Lord triumph, drawing all things to himself.

"In spite of feeling devoid of virtue and knowledge (humility is truth . . . without exaggeration), I would like to write books of fire—books that will race across the world like burning flames and set people ablaze with their light and heat, turning poor hearts into red-hot coals to be offered to Jesus as rubies for his royal crown."

Handwriting of Saint Josemaría: "contemplative souls in the midst of the world."

Saints in Ordinary Life

"Since 1928 I have understood clearly that God wants our Lord's whole life to be an example for Christians. I saw this with special reference to his hidden life, the years he spent working side by side with ordinary men. Our Lord wants many people to ratify their vocation during years of quiet, unspectacular living. . . . I want to shout out to them this divine truth: if you are there in the middle of ordinary life, it doesn't mean Christ has forgotten about you or hasn't called you. He has invited you to stay among the activities and concerns of the world. He wants you to know that your human vocation, your profession, your talents, are not outside his divine plans. He has sanctified them and made them a most pleasing offering to his Father" (Christ Is Passing By, 20).

THE FIRST YEARS

The task was huge and the young priest had no financial resources, helpers, or patrons. He had neither the support of tradition nor Church approval, for although the basic vision was simple in itself, the institution he was founding would not be easily understood. Certainly he did not lack optimism or confidence that the Work was something from God, but the difficulties were numerous indeed.

As confirmation that the project was His own, God made his presence felt time and again to lay a solid foundation both for the spiritual structure and the people who would work within it. In mid-October, 1931, while in a streetcar he received the gift of an exalted form of prayer. "I felt the action of God, bringing forth in my heart and on my lips, with the force of something imperatively necessary, this tender invocation: *Abba! Pater!* ('Abba! Father!'). . . . Probably I made that prayer out loud. And I walked the streets of Madrid for maybe an hour, maybe two, I can't say; time passed without my being aware of it. People must have thought I was crazy. I was contemplating, with lights that were not mine, that amazing truth. It was like a lighted coal burning in my soul, never to be extinguished."

His spiritual life already characterized by a childlike trust, now saw the mystery of his adoptive sonship in Jesus Christ with extraordinary depth. "I understood that divine filiation had to be a basic characteristic of our spirituality: *Abba, Pater!* And that by living their divine filiation, my children would be filled with joy and peace, protected by an impregnable wall. And they would be apostles of joy, communicating their peace, even in the face of their own or another's suffering. Because we are convinced that God is our Father."

He continued his service to the sick and poor, seeking, in their prayer and suffering offered to God, courage to guide the divine endeavor. Father José María Somoano, one of the priests who accompanied him in assisting the terminally ill, committed himself to Opus Dei. So did Maria Ignacia Garcia Escobar, a young woman with tuberculosis, who died a short time after offering her life for the Work.

Maria Ignacia Garcia Escobar.

Already by 1933 he had gathered around him a group of college students. He met them wherever he could, encouraging them to develop a passionate love of Jesus. He would go out for walks with them

El Sotanillo, *the bar where Josemaría met sometimes with young people, to speak to them about God.*

and often stop in a café called *El Sotanillo* ('little basement'), where over cups of hot chocolate he would reveal his dreams of apostolate in the world. He advised them to read and meditate on books on the life and the passion of Our Lord, writing as a dedication in one of those books:

"+ Madrid, 29 May 1933...May you seek Christ...May you find Christ...May you love Christ."

He invited the students to join him on visits to the needy and the sick, lending a hand with small acts of service. He organized catechism classes in the slum neighborhoods on the outskirts of the capital as a way of getting them to help the poor.

Finally the moment arrived to start courses of formation to transmit the spirit of the Work in a more systematic way. Many were invited to the first meeting at a shelter run by nuns. Only three made it. Content nonetheless, he brought them to the chapel afterwards for Eucharistic Benediction. "When I blessed those three . . . I saw three hundred, three hundred thousand, thirty million, three billion. . . . white, black, yellow, of all the colors, all the combinations that human love can produce. And I fell short . . . because our Lord has been generous beyond my wildest dreams."

In 1930, Isidoro Zorzano, a young engineer, a former schoolmate of Father Josemaría's in Logroño, asked to be admitted to Opus Dei. Others followed suit. The founder felt the urgent need for a place for formation to provide unity and visibility. The apostolic

instrument he had in mind would be a civil entity permeated with a Christian spirit. And so the DYA Academy was begun in 1933. Here supplementary classes in law and architecture were given in an apartment with a plaque on the door with these three letters on it, DYA, the Spanish initials for *Derecho y Arquitectura* (Law and Architecture). But for Father Josemaría and the students, the acronym also held a deeper significance: *Dios y audacia* ("God and daring"). And the daring was not lacking, since it ran on a shoe-string budget.

In reality it was more than an educational initiative. It was a place for the Christian formation of college students, who could also receive spiritual direction, a formation entirely aimed at personal identification with Christ. In the reception room, a black wooden cross (not a crucifix) hung on the wall. If someone wondered what it meant, his explanation was "It is waiting for the crucified figure that it lacks, and that . . . has to be you."

For the following academic year, Father Josemaría wanted to take another step forward: moving to a bigger place that would provide housing for some students. Humanly speaking the financial outlook was dismal. He got everyone to pray and entrusted the matter to God. And by the beginning of the semester they were already working away at the new DYA Academy Residence on Ferraz Street. Without miracles, with a lot of suffering, with a lot of prayer and a lot of faith. *Deo omnis gloria!* he prayed, "to God be all the glory."

In December, 1934 he was named rector of the Royal Foundation of Saint Elizabeth, which included

Saint Josemaría with a group of residents of the DYA Academy.

a convent founded by Saint Alonso de Orozco, of whose Augustinian nuns he was already chaplain.

In these years he began to draw up foundational documents: instructions and lengthy letters delineating the spirit and way of doing apostolate proper to Opus Dei for the generations to come. An example: *"The Work of God comes to fulfill the will of God.* Be convinced that Heaven is committed to seeing it accomplished . . . When our Lord God plans some work for the benefit of human beings, he first thinks of those he will use as his instruments . . . and *gives them the necessary graces.* This supernatural conviction of the divine nature of the enterprise will eventually give you such an intense enthusiasm and love for the Work that you will feel *delighted to sacrifice yourselves to bring it to fulfillment."*

The year 1934 also saw the publication of thoughts for meditation entitled *Spiritual Considerations,* which years later, with some additions and editing, would become *The Way.* These points aimed at renewing the Christian life of young people, students and workers, guiding them to a truly contemplative life.

In July, 1935, Álvaro del Portillo, a highly gifted engineering student, asked for admission to Opus Dei. He would become Escrivá's closest collaborator and after the founder's death would be elected to lead Opus Dei.

Meanwhile Spain suffered a series of crises of various sorts. Religious persecution by extremist groups became ever more bold and violent, with the burning of Churches and convents and the murder of priests and religious.

Saint Josemaría Escrivá and Alvaro del Portillo.

Unity of Life

"To unite work with ascetical struggle and contemplation could seem impossible, but it is necessary if the world is to be reconciled with God. This daily toil is to be converted into a means of personal sanctification and apostolate. Is not this a noble and grand ideal for which it is worth giving up one's life?" (Saint Josemaría Escrivá, cited in The Canonical Path of Opus Dei, p. 37).

THE CIVIL WAR

August 30, 1936. For a bit more than a month Spain has been split into two factions, increasingly squaring off in a fratricidal war. The life of Father Josemaría, like that of so many other priests, is at risk. He moves from one hiding place to another. Militiamen hang a man who looks like him, right in front of his mother's house, thinking that it was he. Now he is in the home of some friends, together with Juan—one of the first members of the Work—and a young man he met only two days previously. About two in the afternoon, a group of soldiers, sweeping the neighborhood in an intense manhunt for enemies, rings the bell. Catholics, especially priests and religious, are prime targets. The voice of the elderly maid answering the door is loud enough to be heard all over the house:

"Oh! You must be here for the search and requisition . . . The owner isn't here, but make yourselves at home!

The three guests scamper up the service stairway and take refuge in an attic. The space is narrow, low-ceilinged, soot-filled, without ventilation. They crouch behind some old furniture. Time drags on silently and interminably. The heat becomes unbearable. Now they hear the soldiers approaching. At the end of the methodical search they arrive at the top floor and enter the room next door. The Father whispers to the two youths:

"We're in a tight spot. If you wish, make an act of contrition while I give the absolution."

He absolves them. Juan asks him,

"Father, and if they kill us, what will happen?"

"Why, we'll go right to heaven, my son."

Juan finds the thought so comforting that he falls asleep.

The other two hear meticulous rummaging in the next room. Now it's time for their hiding place . . .

But no. Instead the soldiers descend the stairway and vanish. The fugitives heave a sigh of relief, but stay put until nine in the evening, until after the

The notebook in which Father Josemaría wrote the text of the Mass of the Blessed Virgin Mary which he used when he crossed the Pyrenees.

main gate to the patio of the apartment building is closed. They are sweaty, dehydrated, dirty. One of the youths goes down to one of the apartments:

"Please, could you give me a glass of water?"

The maid, startled, allows him to enter.

"Upstairs there are two more persons."

"Well then, tell them to come down right now!"

They are able to wash up and change clothes. The Father smiles, drawing a moral from the incident:

"Until today I never knew the value of a glass of water!"

They gladly accept the hospitality offered by the woman. The next day the soldiers continue to scour the building. Frequently they knock on the door for help with one thing or another; each time she trembles with fear. She suggests saying the rosary, and the Father takes her up on it, not hiding his identity:

"I'll lead it. I'm a priest."

A day later he thanks his hosts, but tells them that he is leaving immediately in order not to be a danger for them or compromise their situation.

Once again a desperate search for yet another place of refuge, none really safer than the last.

* * *

With the outbreak of the war, the few members of Opus Dei were forced to scatter. The Father—as he had come to be called familiarly by his spiritual sons—moved from one shelter to another, always in danger. With heroic fortitude he declined a few secure hiding places that were unsuited to his priestly condition. At times the safest place was the street, where he walked from morning until night blending into the crowd.

In the midst of this he continued to celebrate Mass when possible and to provide priestly assistance to many, besides the members of the Work, whom he was able to contact. He even preached a retreat by setting up a series of appointments in unlikely places. News arrived of martyred priests, friends of his.

For a number of months he found temporary

December 3, 1937 in Andorra: Father Josemaría and the group that had crossed the border over the Pyrenees.

haven in a psychiatric clinic, feigning madness with the complicity of its director, Dr. Suils. At last he was able to obtain entrance for himself and several companions at the consulate of Honduras. Its diplomatic status guaranteed a modicum of safety. Sites such as this one were packed with refugees, food was scarce, the atmosphere depressed and tense. Father Josemaría drew up a schedule for his young followers, had them devote time to study, preached to them, and even discreetly reserved the Blessed Sacrament in a small desk. His great joy was being able to celebrate Mass every day. The engineer Isidoro Zorzano, who could move about freely because of his Argentine citizenship, served as a means of contacting those outside the consulate.

A sketch of Father Josemaría done during the flight across the Pyrenees.

But how long would this war go on? When would the persecution end? How long could he be stuck in this situation, without being able to begin the expansion of the Work? He thought it over and consulted with the young men who followed him. Yes, it was necessary to cross over to the other part of Spain where a normal Christian life was possible. The only practical way, although it held no guarantee of success, was to cross the Pyrenees and get there by way of France. It was September 1937.

It would have been very easy for anyone in his place to ask himself why so many difficulties were arising to block a project that was clearly divine. Why did God permit such obstacles? But the young priest, who from the time of his childhood had learned to swallow the bitterness of deep sorrow, was already an expert in the science of the Cross. It was not resignation, but deep understanding of the path of suffering, since it was on the cross that Christ triumphed and saved us. He was convinced of this all his life. Thus he wrote, referring to himself, "When you celebrated the feast of the Exaltation of the Holy Cross you asked our Lord, with the most earnest desire of your heart, to grant you his grace so as to 'exalt' the Holy Cross in the powers of your soul and in your senses. You asked for a new life; for the Cross to set a seal on it, to confirm the truth of your mission; for the whole of your being to rest on the Cross!"

Yet it was not an easy decision for the founder.

The idea of leaving some of his people and his mother with his brother and sister behind in wartime Madrid tormented him. Nevertheless he realized the urgency of carrying on with the apostolate that he knew to be the will of God. And for better or worse, on the other side of the battle front he could do that.

With improvised documentation he arrived in Barcelona on October 10, 1937. This was the city from which "convoys" of refugees departed, guided by mountaineers and smugglers—all undercover, as the circumstances required. He and those with him had to wait, hungry and with almost no spending money, for about a month until a convoy could be organized.

Traversing mountains by foot, in late-autumn chill, walking by night and hiding by day, without equipment of any type, with the physical weakness resulting from months of deprivation, in constant danger of being discovered and shot . . . this was a tall order for anyone, especially for persons already tested by a war both too long and inhumane. The stages of

the escape were numerous and rough. At times, they waited for days in some outpost, at the guide's orders. Father Josemaría introduced himself as a priest right away and celebrated Mass whenever possible. The last of these Masses, in the shelter of a grotto, kneeling for the whole celebration before an altar of rock, moved the entire group: "Never have I heard a Mass like the one today. I don't know if it is due to the circumstances or because the priest is a saint," wrote one of those present.

On December 2, good fortune allowed them to cross the border of Andorra. They were exhausted but safe. A heavy snowstorm stranded them in Andorra for several days. But at last they could resume the journey through France, with a stop at Lourdes to thank our Lady. When they crossed back into Spain at Hendaye, Father Josemaría recited a Hail Holy Queen.

Wooden rose which he found in Rialp, in the Pyrenees, and took as a sign of our Lady's protection.

BEGINNING AGAIN

The so-called "Nationalist" zone of Spain during the war had established its provisional capital in Burgos. There government officials, civil servants, and many other people were waiting to return to their cities, among them Church officials. Beyond any political considerations, there was a rekindling of religious fervor there, perhaps in response to persecution.

After crossing the Pyrenees, the founder settled in Burgos, taking a room in a modest inn, the Hotel Sabadell. From this base he undertook an intense apostolate. First he had to track down the persons he knew before the war and continue their formation. He spared no effort to see them, traveling with almost no funds, enduring the discomfort brought on by the devastation of war. Some used their precious furloughs to come to see him in Burgos

Father Josemaría encouraged all of them to think with broader horizons. The young men yearned for these meetings. "We used to go for walks along the banks of the River Arlanzón. There we would talk, and while they opened their hearts, I tried to guide them with suitable advice to confirm their decisions or open up new horizons in their interior lives. And always, with God's help, I would do all I could to encourage them and stir up in their hearts the desire to live genuinely Christian lives. Our walks would sometimes take us as far as the abbey of Las Huelgas. On other occasions we would find our way to the cathedral.

"I used to enjoy climbing up the cathedral towers to get a close view of the ornamentation at the top, a veritable lacework of stone that must have been the result of very patient and laborious craftsmanship. As I chatted with the young men who accompanied me I used to point out that none of the beauty of this work could be seen from below. To give them a material lesson in what I had been previously explaining to them, I would say: 'This is God's work, this is working for God! To finish your personal work perfectly, with all the beauty and exquisite refinement of this tracery stonework.'"

Father Josemaría dreamed of a great expansion of Opus Dei, of a fruitful service to the Church. Already he was thinking of preparing some of the young men to send to other countries. "Night was falling as you and I began our prayer. From close by came the murmur of water. And, through the stillness of the city, we also seemed to hear voices of people from many lands, crying to us in anguish that they do not yet know Christ. Unashamedly you kissed your crucifix and you asked him to make you an apostle of apostles."

He traveled to speak about the Work with many bishops, who received him cordially and encouraged him. He collected liturgical objects and whatever else might be useful in beginning again in Madrid as soon as it would be possible. Above all, he sought books from whoever could give them. These young men would have to be well prepared to carry Christ to the various fields of knowledge and culture.

And as always, he preached by his example. Since the material for his doctoral thesis back in Madrid had been lost in the war, he began another line of research on the abbey of Las Huelgas, an institution with an unusual and interesting type of jurisdiction in canon law.

The plaque found among the ruins of the DYA Academy.

He sent out a torrent of correspondence to keep in contact with all the people with whom he had ties, especially his spiritual sons. He wrote brief letters, incisive and paternal. But how long would he have to endure this waiting? He seasoned his desire to get moving with formidable mortifications, penances and fasts, and the resolution to abandon all concerns about money to our Lord. With the meager income that they could put together by pooling resources, they had barely enough to live on.

Finally the moment arrived: they could return to Madrid. His holy impatience led him to enter the capital with the first military convoy that moved into the city. He was the first priest to return; it was March 28, 1939. The student academy/residence, which had cost him so much sacrifice, appeared to be completely destroyed. In an emotional moment he retrieved from the rubble a framed inscription of the words which Jesus himself in the Gospel had defined as the new commandment and as the sign by which his disciples would be recognized: "That you love one another, even as I have loved you . . ."

Beginning again. A spirit of hope and sacrifice completely beyond the ordinary led him to open another residence. He moved his family there as well. His mother and sister took charge of managing the household tasks, and to this is owed, in good part, the family tone that can be found to this day in all the centers of Opus Dei.

In June he preached a retreat for students near Valencia, which gave a big lift to the work of Opus Dei in that city. Also in Valencia, *The Way* was published in September. A number of people began to arrive who wished to give themselves to God by committing themselves completely to Opus Dei. Although the difficult situation in Europe at the outset of World War II required postponement of plans for international development, expansion to other parts of Spain continued.

March 28, 1939, Father Josemaría among the ruins of the DYA Academy.

Apostolate

"Don't let your life be barren. Be useful. Blaze a trail. Shine forth with the torch of your faith and your love.

"With your apostolic life, wipe out the trail of filth and slime left by the corrupt sowers of hatred. And set aflame all the ways of the earth with the fire of Christ that you bear in your heart" (The Way, no. 1).

HELPING PRIESTS

"I began to give many, many retreats—they used to last seven days at that time—in a number of Spanish dioceses. I was very young and it embarrassed me. I always began by going to our Lord and saying to him: 'You'll have to see what you are going to say to your priests, because I . . .' I felt so awkward! And afterwards if they didn't come to chat, I called them one by one, because they weren't used to talking to the preacher."

At the beginning of the 1940's many bishops asked Father Josemaría to preach to their clergy. After the devastation of the civil war it was necessary to nourish the spiritual life of priests, and the laity as well. Father Josemaría's reputation was growing, not only as an excellent preacher, but also as a holy priest. Some years the number of priests making these retreats exceeded one thousand.

His preaching was his personal prayer made out loud. To his listeners he conveyed his love for our Lord, his own interior life. His theme was always Jesus and the good news of the Gospel, reflecting on Christ's life in vivid terms. Whatever his immediate topic, whether sin or grace or eternal life, his destination was always personal union with Jesus who lives and who loves us.

His love for the priesthood and for priests was transparent. In 1941, when he had to leave town for

A moment in the preaching of St. Josemaría, at that time rather overweight because of his diabetes.

one of these retreats, in Lérida, his mother was ill. He decided to go anyway, because the doctor did not think it was serious.

"Could you offer your sufferings for the work I'm going to do?" he asked her.

As he left the room he heard her murmur:

"This son of mine . . ."

Arriving at the seminary of Lérida, he had knelt before the tabernacle, saying:

"Lord, look after my mother, for I am taking care of your priests."

Two days later, the thought of his mother still very much in his heart, he proceeded to preach on the role of the priest's mother. It occurred to him to tell his listeners that her role was so important that she should not die till the day after the death of her son the priest.

After the meditation he remained recollected in prayer in front of the Blessed Sacrament. Then the apostolic administrator of the diocese, who was making the retreat, came up to him somewhat disconcerted and said in a low voice:

"Álvaro del Portillo would like you to phone him in Madrid."

His mother, Dolores, had died.

Years later, Saint Josemaría affirmed, "I have always thought that our Lord wanted that sacrifice from me, as an external proof of my love for diocesan priests, and that my mother especially continues to intercede for that work."

That work, like all his activity, was carried out in close union with the bishops. The prelates held him in high regard and blessed the apostolate he was doing with students and other persons in every walk of life.

The bishop of Madrid, the Most Reverend Leopoldo Eijo y Garay, grasped the nature and mission of Opus Dei, and with paternal and seemingly limitless affection he felt honored to facilitate its development in any way possible. His relationship with Father Josemaría was one of firm mutual trust.

However, the Work in general and the founder

Handwriting of Saint Josemaría: "a great mission of ours is to make people love the religious."

in particular ran up against the misunderstandings of certain clerics. It didn't take long for a full-blown campaign of rumors and even calumnies to start. Father Josemaría suffered and forgave.

The good bishop, seriously concerned, wished to grant diocesan approval to Opus Dei in March, 1941, hoping to put an end to the malicious gossip. "One night when I was in bed and beginning to fall asleep (when I slept, I slept very soundly; I never lost sleep over the slanders, persecutions and falsehoods of those times) the telephone rang. I answered and heard 'Josemaría . . .' It was Don Leopoldo, then bishop of Madrid. There was a special warmth in his voice . . . 'What is it?' I asked. And he said to me, *'Ecce Satanas expetivit vos ut cribaret sicut triticum'* ('Behold, Satan demanded to have you, that he might sift you like wheat' [*Lk* 22:31]). Then he added: 'I pray so much for you all . . . *Et tu . . . confirma filios tuos!'* ('You, confirm your sons'). And he hung up."

Father Josemaría did everything he could to avoid harboring resentment and to forgive. One night in 1942, exasperated with a heavy load of work and wagging gossiping tongues, he knelt before the tabernacle and declared:

"Lord, if you don't need my honor, why should I want it?"

The faithful of the Work multiplied to the point that providing priestly ministry to all of them became a concern. Father Josemaría knew that the priests should come from among the laity of Opus Dei. But as much as the founder racked his brain for a solution, he could not find a path that solved the canonical problem of the title of ordination of the future priests.

As always, it was God who furnished the solution. The morning of February 14, 1943, while he celebrated Mass in a center of Opus Dei, our Lord let him see the solution clearly and precisely. After the Mass he sketched out the seal of the Work (the cross in the world) and began to speak of the Priestly Society of the Holy Cross.

Already three of the first members of Opus Dei, all engineers, had been preparing for priestly ordination. On June 25, 1944 they received Holy Orders at the hands of the bishop of Madrid. Father

Josemaría with the first three faithful of Opus Dei who later would be ordained as priests.

Josemaría did not want to be present at what could appear to be a success or a triumph. He stayed at home, praying. As he put it in writing some years later: "My role is to hide and disappear, so that only Jesus shines forth."

However, his concern for the diocesan clergy, so obvious in those years in which he spent so much time in their pastoral care, never dissipated. Couldn't they too be part of Opus Dei? The eventual inclusion of diocesan priests would have to overcome hurdles posed by canon law that seemed difficult to solve. So strong was his yearning to provide adequate spiritual assistance to diocesan clergy that in 1950 he planned to launch a foundation separate from the Work for this purpose. It would turn out not to be necessary. Our Lord inspired him once more: diocesan priests could be incorporated into the Priestly Society of the Holy Cross, while remaining entirely subject to the bishop of the diocese in which they were incardinated.

TRAVELING TO ROME

Stepping out on the sixth floor balcony of an apartment on the Piazza della Città Leonina which some of his sons were renting, Father Josemaría realized how close it was to the Papal apartments—as the crow flies. Only the street and the lower

During his first days in Rome.

barracks of the Swiss guard separated him from them. Night was falling and through the windows of rooms in the Apostolic Palace, where the lights were still on, he could almost glimpse the profile of Pius XII. Deeply moved, he ended up spending the entire night on the terrace keeping prayerful vigil for the Holy Father.

What a flood of memories! In Madrid, in the time of Pius XI, he had made the rounds from one part of the city to another reciting the Rosary, at the end of which he imagined himself receiving Communion from the hands of the Pope. The Pope had become one of his three great loves, together with Christ and Mary. And now . . . he was here. It was the night spanning June 23–24, 1946. The gentle Roman dawn found him still on the terrace, physically exhausted, but with an ineffable spiritual joy.

Worn out, indeed, because he had arrived in Rome that afternoon after an event-filled journey.

The Work, now beyond its infancy, needed Papal approval to guarantee the secularity of its faithful, and the unity and universality of its apostolates in all the dioceses of the world. Diocesan approval was not enough. But what structure under canon law would take its place? The canon law then in force did not provide a formula suited to this new pastoral phenomenon—ordinary Christians who seek holiness in the middle of the world through their professional work. Álvaro del Portillo, representing the founder, had traveled to Rome twice and had made some headway, but he found the doors closed. The Work, they told him, had come one hundred years too soon. The situation called for the presence of the founder . . .

But Father Josemaría was gravely ill. Since at least 1944 he had been suffering from an acute form of diabetes. "The doctors felt," he said at the time, "that I could die at any moment. When I went to bed, I did not know if I would get up again. And when I got up in the morning I didn't know if I

The ship in which he made the journey from Barcelona to Genoa in 1946.

would last until the evening." The doctor in charge, a noted specialist, declared "I cannot answer for your life," if the trip to Rome was made. But he needed to make it, and he did.

He went to Barcelona to embark there for Genoa. In the Catalonian capital he got together with his sons and preached a meditation to them. It was not his health that worried him, but the canonical future of the Work. "Lord, could you have allowed me to deceive so many souls in good faith, when I've done it all for your glory, knowing it was your will? Is it possible that the Holy See will say that we've arrived a century too soon? Behold we have left all things and followed you! I never wanted to deceive anybody. I never wanted to do anything

other than serve you. Is there any possibility that I could be a fraud?" The Barcelona contingent listened with emotion. Hounded by slander, they had already learned from the founder to put their trust completely in God's providence.

Together with a young student of legal history, José Orlandis, he embarked on the steamship J. J. Sister. In the Gulf of Lyons, a furious storm hammered the boat for 20 hours. In addition to a real possibility of shipwreck, practically all aboard, from the captain to the last passenger, became seasick. And Father Josemaría was already gravely ill. Not entirely joking, he commented to his companion:

"It appears that the devil does not want us to get to Rome!"

But finally they reached Genoa, where Father Álvaro was waiting to take them to Rome by car, amidst the discomforts of a country only beginning to recover from World War II. And there in Rome he discovered how close he was to the Pope's home . . . Shortly afterwards he told a churchman about that night in prayer, and in no time found that word of it had spread around, and that some were laughing at him behind his back. "At first this murmuring hurt me, but it made a love for the Roman Pontiff that was less 'Spanish,' i.e. less emotional, arise in my heart—born of more solid, more theological reflection, and therefore more profound. Since then I've always said that 'in Rome I lost my innocence,' and this event has been most useful for my soul."

Father Álvaro was right: the presence of the founder hastened the complicated process of approvals. The first warm words of encouragement were from Monsignor Giovanni Battista Montini, the future Pope Paul VI, who always showed Josemaría Escrivá friendship and kindness. Pius XII

received him in audience after a few weeks. He had spoken with other members of Opus Dei already, but was impressed by the founder. Later on he confided to Cardinal Gilroy:

"He is a true saint, a man sent by God for our times." And in fact it was Pius XII who gave Opus Dei the pontifical approvals toward which it had been working, the first in 1947 and then more definitively in 1950. These approvals created a legal framework under Church law, which though admittedly imperfect, was necessary for minimal stability.

Many cardinals, bishops, and prelates visited the tiny apartment of Cittá Leonina. His theologically-rooted love for the Pope would last and grow throughout his entire life. And in response, the warmth and esteem of the Popes toward Opus Dei grew. John XXIII had already been introduced to the spirit of Opus Dei when he visited a university residence in 1950 in Santiago de Compostela and stayed briefly in a center in Saragossa. Saint Josemaría's first audience with the new Pope was on March 5, 1960.

The following Pope, Paul VI dealt with him with fatherly affection. "We look with paternal satis-faction," said the Pope in 1964, "on how much Opus Dei has done and continues to do for the Kingdom of God, the desire for the good that guides it, the fervent love of the Church and her visible head which distinguishes it, the ardent zeal for souls which impels it along arduous and difficult paths of apostolate of presence and witness in all sectors of contemporary life." The Pope had the opportunity to meet the founder on numerous occasions and to express his conviction that he was a saint.

"When you are old," the Father told members of Opus Dei, "and I have already rendered my ac-count to God, you will tell your brothers and sisters how the Father loved the Pope with all his soul, with all his strength."

*Above,
with Blessed
John XXIII.*

*On the left,
a photo
dedicated by
Pope Pius XII and
Msgr. Giovanni
Battista Montini,
the future Pope
Paul VI.*

JOY, SORROW, HOPE

From the earliest days of his apostolic work, Saint Josemaría had emphasized the dignity of marriage, strongly pointing out that it is a divine vocation and a call to sanctity. Already in *The Way* he had written: "You laugh because I tell you that you have a 'vocation to marriage?' —Well, you have: just that, a vocation. Commend yourself to Saint Raphael, so that he may lead you chastely to the end of the journey, as he did Tobias."

And in *Christ Is Passing By* we read: "Christian marriage is not just a social institution, much less a mere remedy for human weakness. It is a real supernatural calling. A great sacrament, in Christ and in the Church, says St. Paul. At the same time it is a permanent contract between a man and a woman. Whether we like it or not, the sacrament of matrimony, instituted by Christ, cannot be dissolved. It is a permanent contract that sanctifies in cooperation with Jesus Christ. He fills the souls of husband and wife and invites them to follow him. He transforms their whole married life into an occasion for God's presence on earth. Husband and wife are called to sanctify their married life and to sanctify themselves in it."

With a group of young women, in Rome.

Hence the Father's joy when he discovered the canonical way for married people to join Opus Dei. As soon as possible, he organized a retreat at Molinoviejo, not far from Madrid, for the persons who had been waiting for this, so that they could prepare spiritually to form part of Opus Dei.

In addition to the joys, there were sorrows as well. It was precisely as a consequence of the approval of Opus Dei in 1950, and in spite of Pius XII's public approval, that a very serious move was made against the Work and its founder. Some persons—with great influence in the Curia—attempted to expel the founder from the Work and to divide his sons and daughters in a way that would denature their path in the Church.

The founder was in the dark about the intrigue. But with the instinct of a father and a mother, he intuited that something very harmful was about to befall him and Opus Dei. He confided to his children in Rome, "I feel like a blind man who has to defend himself, but can only beat the air with his cane: I don't know what is going on, but something is afoot . . ."

"All things work for good for those who love God." (Rom 8, 28). By express indication of Saint Josemaría, this inscription in Latin was painted on the walls of the house where he lived in Rome.

Not knowing whom he could turn to on earth, he had recourse, as always, to heaven. He decided to make a penitential pilgrimage to the shrine of Loreto to consecrate the Work to our Lady. It was penitential indeed due to the torrid heat and the irritations stemming from his poor health. Kneeling in the Holy House after having celebrated Mass, he entrusted Opus Dei to Mary, invoking her motherly protection. On his return he regained his peace and serenity. From that time on he often repeated, and encouraged others to repeat, the aspiration *Cor Mariae dulcissimum, iter para tutum!* ("Most sweet heart of Mary, prepare a safe way for us").

The answer from heaven was not long in coming. A few months later, the archbishop of Milan, Cardinal Schuster (today *Blessed* Cardinal Schuster), who had taken the budding apostolate of Opus Dei in his city very much to heart, called Father Giovanni Udaondo. "How is your founder doing?"

"He's very well!" he replied, not aware of anything amiss.

"But how does he carry his cross? Doesn't he have to bear the burden of some specific setback, a very heavy cross?"

"Well, if that's the case, he would be very happy, because he has always taught us that, if we stand close to the Cross, we stand very close to Jesus."

"Tell him to be alert. Let him remember his countryman Saint Joseph Calasanz, as well as Saint Alphonsus Liguori . . . and get moving!"

The warning was clear. Both saints had endured heavy persecutions. The founder visited many important prelates, but it seemed as if no one knew anything about it. Finally he got Cardinal Tedeschini to carry a letter from him directly to Pius XII. The Pope read it on March 18, 1952 and stopped the plan dead in its tracks.

Saint Josemaría would eventually come to know who was behind the intrigue. But he did not divulge it; he did not want anything to leak out to his daughters and sons, fearing that it might lead to a lack of charity. He wished only to pardon. He was convinced that these persons, like others who had earlier attacked the Work, had done it *obsequium se putantes praestare Deum,* "thinking they were serving God." He was convinced that for some people it was not easy to understand the theological and pastoral novelty of Opus Dei and for this reason they should be given the benefit of the doubt even

Father Josemaría with two of his sons from Ireland and Ecuador.

when, in opposing something that they understood poorly or did not understand at all, they acted badly. In short, the Work went ahead defended, but pardoning its detractors.

Many years later he confided to his children: "Do you know why the Work has developed so much? Because they have treated it like a sack of wheat; it's been beaten and battered about. But the seeds are so small that they haven't broken. On the contrary, they've been scattered to the four winds; they've landed wherever there have been hearts hungry and ready for the truth. And now we have so many vocations and we are a very large family, and there are millions of souls who admire and love the Work because they see in it a sign of God's presence among men, and recognize the inexhaustible riches of his mercy." Years of voluntary seclusion followed. The founder needed to govern the expansion of the Work, fighting the "battle of formation" of his sons and daughters.

The recourse to supernatural means was a constant characteristic of Saint Josemaría. As a sign of his unshakable faith in God in big and little matters, he wished to consecrate Opus Dei on several occasions besides the one previously mentioned. On May 14, 1951, as a result of the misunderstanding that existed among some parents in Rome, he decided to consecrate the families of the members of the Work to the Holy Family of Nazareth.

". . . O Jesus, our most lovable Redeemer," reads the text of this consecration, "Who in coming to enlighten the world with Your example and doctrine, chose to spend the greater part of Your life subject to Mary and Joseph in the humble house in Nazareth, sanctifying the Family that all Christian homes were to imitate; graciously accept the consecration of the families of Your children in Opus Dei, which we now make to You. Take them under Your protection and care, and fashion them after the divine model of Your holy Family."

Divine Filiation

"This divine filiation is the basis of the spirit of Opus Dei. All men are children of God. But a child can look upon his father in many ways. We must try to be children who realize that the Lord, by loving us as his children, has taken us into his house, in the middle of the world, to be members of his family, so that what is his is ours, and what is ours is his, and to develop that familiarity and confidence which prompts us to ask him, like children, for the moon!"
(Christ Is Passing By, 64).

EXPANSION

The Father's diabetes was the cause of great discomfort. He lived with a constant headache, suffered chronic thirst, and gained too much weight, in addition to the other problems that can arise in connection with this illness. Each day he was injected with a heavy dose of insulin. But his attitude remained one of unfailing cheerfulness. He joked with good humor about the excess sugar in his blood:

"I guess they'll have to call me *Pater dulcissimus* ('Most Sweet Father')."

He seemed to give no importance to the incurable nature of the disease.

On April 27, 1954 Fr. Álvaro had just given him an injection of insulin and they were seated at a table. All of a sudden, the Father asked him:

"Álvaro, give me absolution."

Fr. Álvaro, failing to understand him, replied:

"But Father, what are you talking about?"

"Absolution!"

During the construction work at Villa Tevere.

Seeing his confusion, the Father began to prompt him with the sacramental words:

"Ego te absolvo . . . " ("I absolve you . . . ")

He lost consciousness, fell on one side and immediately began to turn different colors: red, purple, clammy yellow . . .

Fr. Álvaro gave him absolution and hurriedly called the doctor, but by the time he arrived, the Father was already coming to. It had been an anaphylactic shock. He was left blind for several hours, but afterwards recovered completely. Although some of the consequences of the disease would remain with him in the years to come, he no longer had diabetes. The attending physician was dumbfounded. The sickness had lasted more than ten years.

By this time, the property in Rome, on Bruno Buozzi Avenue, had become a construction site. They had obtained the property as usual with almost no funds, confiding in the providence of God and with the encouragement of various Curia officials. At the beginning they had to live in the small gatehouse at the entrance called the pensionato, whose tenants had moved out. Now the house started taking shape. A house which would never be rich, the founder said, but which would be built to last, precisely out of love for poverty: Villa Tevere.

These years were also the years of the spread of the Work in Europe and the Americas. In 1946 some members of Opus Dei began working in Portugal, Italy, and Great Britain. In 1947 it was France and Ireland's turn. By the end of the decade a start had been made in Mexico and the United States. In 1950, Chile and Argentina; in 1951, Colombia and Venezuela, in 1952, Germany. The expansion would continue at this lively pace. By 1949 a summer course of formation was held for the first members from various countries.

Handwriting of Saint Josemaría on the first letter of his children from Japan.

The Work took hardy root in these diverse locales, a sign that it was God's doing. And people began to come to the Work in all of these places, from very different cultural and social backgrounds. The need to furnish them with a more effective formation arose. Thus, in 1948, although still hampered by makeshift living arrangements, Saint

Josemaría established the Roman College of the Holy Cross. To it would come members of the Work from all over the world for a special period of formation close to the heart of the Church and the heart of the Work.

On December 12, 1953 he established the Roman College of Saint Mary for the women of Opus Dei. Since that time thousands of men and women have been formed in these centers. Many of the men who studied there have received priestly ordination.

Another forward-looking innovation of these years was to admit non-Catholics as cooperators. "With respect to religious freedom, from its foundation Opus Dei has never practiced discrimination of any kind. It works and lives with everyone because it sees in each person a soul which must be respected and loved. These are not mere words. Our Work . . . with the authorization of the Holy See, admitted non-Catholics, whether Christian or not, as Cooperators." This is why Saint Josemaría could jokingly, but with great respect, say to Pope John XXIII: "I did not learn ecumenism from Your Holiness," because non-Catholics, including non-Christians, were already cooperators of the Work prior to his pontificate.

The founder sent his sons and daughters to various countries with the same faith in Providence with which he had begun every activity—with almost nothing, as Jesus sent out his disciples. But he followed their steps with fatherly care. He undertook long and uncomfortable trips to visit them and to prepare the terrain (with prayer and meetings with Church authorities) before their arrival. Sister Lucia, the visionary of Fatima, had already asked him in 1945 to have the Work start in Portugal as soon as possible. In 1949 Cardinal Faulhaber of Munich received him enthusiastically, asking that Opus Dei start in Germany. The scene was repeated in Zurich, Basel, Bonn, Cologne, Paris, Amsterdam, Louvain, and other cities. He arrived in Vienna when Soviet soldiers were still a common sight in the streets. There in the Austrian capital he began to

Handwriting of Saint Josemaría: "Sancta Maria, Stella Orientis, filios tuos adiuva! Roma, 14-IV-1959." ("Holy Mary, Star of the East, help your children! Rome, April 14, 1959.")

pray the aspiration *Sancta Maria, Stella Orientis, filios tuos adiuva!* ("Holy Mary, Star of the East, help your children!"), thinking of those countries left under Communist rule after World War II.

He traveled in an antiquated and cramped car on roads still damaged from the recent war, but he lightened the journey for his companions by breaking out into songs and by his cheerful conversation. Often he prayed out loud in the car, commenting on the words of the Lord: "I have chosen you and appointed you that you should go and bear fruit, and that your fruit should abide." Visits to shrines of our Lady were a standard feature of the trip.

In the years straddling the decades of the 1950's and 60's he went to England to spend some weeks during the summer. He placed particular hope in that nation, due both to its university tradition and to its eminent place in the world. "This England is a great place," he wrote. "If you help us, we will work with constancy in this crossroads of the world: pray and offer small mortifications cheerfully."

In August of 1958 he was walking through the city of London, looking at the concentration of powerful institutions built up over centuries. How would it be possible to bring the light of Jesus Christ here? The spirit of the Work? That teeming flow of

With the parents of an Irish son of his.

people of every race and nation, was it really Christian? It seemed as if everything was still left to do, and he felt the weight of all his weakness.

"I can't do it, Lord, I can't do it!"

But God made him understand, "You can't do it, but I can."

However numerous, these forays abroad were always brief. He did not want to be too distant from the headquarters of Opus Dei. His days for the most part were spent in prayer, in reviewing apostolic plans, in forming his sons and daughters. His usual schedule did not vary much during all his years in Rome. Orderly by nature as well as by habit, he knew how to multiply his time. He got up early in the morning, made a half hour of mental prayer with a group of his sons, celebrated Mass—the center and root, not only of his day, but of his life as well. During a breakfast that was frugal even by continental European standards, he glanced at the newspaper, a time that came to be, paradoxically, one of intense union with God, full of thanksgiving and reparation.

Together with Father Alvaro, the secretary general of Opus Dei, he then set to work on the ordinary affairs involved in governing Opus Dei. News, consultations, apostolic plans poured in from all over the world, and the founder had a stated policy of not being the one to hold things up.

At the end of the morning he often received visitors who sought him out for his prayer, his advice, and his affection. People from all over the world, members of the Work or not, came to see him. And all left comforted. After the main meal at mid-day, simple and frugal, he relaxed by getting together with and talking informally with his closest collaborators or with the students of the Roman College. Then he returned to work, prayer, the recitation of the Rosary, study, and writing.

Contemplatives in the Middle of the World

"Our being children of God, I insist, leads us to have a contemplative spirit in the midst of all human activities; to be light, salt and leaven through our prayer, through our mortification, through our knowledge of religion and of our profession. We will carry out this aim: the more within the world we are, the more we must be God's" (The Forge, 740).

THE APOSTOLATE OF THE MIND

"We have to try to ensure that in all fields of intellectual activity there are upright people, people with a true Christian conscience, who are consistent in their lives, who can use the weapons of knowledge in the service of humanity and the Church. Because in the world there will always be, as there were when Jesus came on earth, new Herods who try to make use of knowledge—even if they have to falsify it—to persecute Christ and those who belong to him. What a great task we have ahead of us!"

This was one of his great ideals: the apostolate of the mind, to bring scientists, artists, writers, and intellectuals to Christ.

Granted, his founding vision included people of all types. And his first followers were diverse: students, workers, artists. He had always said, "Of a hundred souls, we are interested in a hundred." The reality of Opus Dei, whose faithful are of the most different cultures, races, trades, professional specializations, and social classes, confirms this criterion of the Founder. "Wherever an honest person can live, that's where we can find air to breathe! That's where we have to be with our joy, with our interior peace, with our desire to bring souls to Christ. Where, you may ask? Among the professions? Among the professions. Among manual workers? Among manual workers. And which of those occupations is better? I will tell you what I have always said: the best work is the one done with most love of God. And you, when you do your work and help your friend, your colleague, your neighbor, in a way that isn't noticed, you are Christ who heals, you are Christ who dwells with mankind."

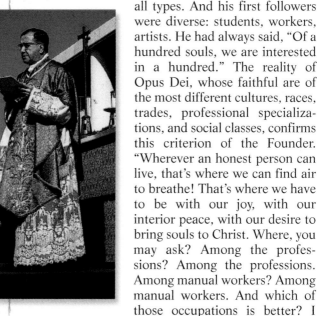

Pamplona, October 8, 1967, while preaching the homily "Passionately Loving the World."

However, the particular influence that intellectuals exercise in steering a country's culture was not lost on him. They may or may not be famous, but they are very influential. He likened them to the masses of perpetual snow on the distant mountain peaks. Though they may be too far away to see, they send the steady stream that waters the fields and makes them fruitful. They are a key element, then, for the Christianization of temporal realities and of society as a whole.

From the time of his studies in law at Saragossa, Saint Josemaría never lost contact with the university world. He encouraged many young people to take up careers as university professors. He encouraged everyone to a serious and profound study of their own field, and an equally serious study of the faith.

In 1952, having prepared the way with a lot of prayer, he founded the University of Navarre in Pamplona. He saw it as a center to infuse science and culture with the light of faith. "Every now and then, monotonously sounding like a broken record, some people try to resurrect a supposed incompatibility between faith and science, between human knowledge and divine revelation. But such incompatibility could only arise—and then only apparently—from a misunderstanding of the elements of the problem. If the world has come from God, if he has created man in his image and likeness and given him a spark of divine light, the task of our intellect should be to uncover the divine meaning imbedded in all things by their nature, even if this can be attained only by dint of hard work. And with the light of faith, we also can perceive their supernatural purpose, resulting from the elevation of the natural order to the higher order of grace. We can never be afraid of developing human knowledge, because all intellectual effort, if it is serious, is aimed at truth."

The University of Navarre began to gain prestige as it actively participated in the world of research, while diligently educating its students. In 1967 Monsignor Escrivá celebrated a Mass on campus for the entire university. His homily on that occasion, now famous as "Passionately Loving the World," traced the panorama of sanctification within temporal realities. Also on this occasion he clarified: ". . . the activities which are promoted by Opus Dei as an institution also have these eminently secular characteristics. They are not ecclesiastical activities. They do not in any way represent the hierarchy of the Church. They are the fruit of human, cultural and social initiatives, carried out by citizens who try to make them reflect the Gospel's light and to enkindle them with Christ's love."

Also under his apostolic guidance the University of Piura in Peru was founded in 1969. It would be followed in due course by other university-level institutions all over the world, a lasting sowing of culture enlightened by the Gospel.

At the same time, Josemaría Escrivá gave decisive encouragement to the creation of elementary and secondary schools in which intellectual formation goes hand in hand with spiritual development according to a personalized system that seeks to develop virtues in the students. Parents played their role in developing these schools, by exercising their mission as primary educators. This model represented a new philosophy of education and has spread rapidly throughout the world.

In the same spirit he encouraged the start of agricultural schools, centers for vocational training and trade skills, schools to help improve the skills of women in developing countries, hospitals and medical dispensaries, etc.

During the granting of honorary doctorates by the University of Navarre.

Sanctification of Work

"Work is a participation in the creative work of God. . . . And, moreover, since Christ took it into his hands, work has become for us a redeemed and redemptive reality. Not only is it the background of man's life, it is a means and path of holiness. It is something to be sanctified and something which sanctifies" (Christ Is Passing By, 47).

VATICAN II

On January 25, 1959, Pope John XXIII surprised the world by convening an ecumenical council. The founder of Opus Dei welcomed the news with great hope and asked everyone to pray "for the happy outcome of this great initiative of an ecumenical council."

Some of his sons would take part in it; among them his closest collaborator, Father Álvaro del Portillo. In the years of the council, many council fathers wanted to meet Monsignor Escrivá and hear his views about the matters under discussion.

At the conclusion of the sessions, he was greatly pleased to receive the council's teaching. "One of my greatest joys was to see the Second Vatican Council so clearly proclaim the divine vocation of the laity. Without any boasting, I would say that as far as our spirit is concerned the Council has not meant an invitation to change, but, on the contrary, has confirmed what, with the grace of God, we have been living and teaching for so many years. The principal characteristic of Opus Dei is not a set of techniques or methods of apostolate, nor any specific structures, but a spirit which moves one to sanctify one's ordinary work."

Some examples can shed light on the affinity that Saint Josemaría Escrivá's teaching has with the magisterium of the council. The Dogmatic Constitution on the Church, *Lumen Gentium*, reads, "It is therefore quite clear that all Christians in any state or walk of life are called to the fullness of Christian life and to the perfection of love, and by this holiness a more human manner of life is fostered also in earthly society" (no. 40). The universal call to holiness was the fulcrum of the teaching of the founder of Opus Dei. In a document as far back as 1930, for example, he affirmed: "Holiness is not something for some privileged few. God calls everyone; from everyone He waits for Love: from everyone, wherever they may be; from everyone, whatever may be their state in life, profession, or occupation."

From the beginning he taught that all the faithful have a priestly soul, participating through it in the priesthood of Christ. In a document of March 11, 1940, he wrote: "With a priestly soul, making the Holy Mass the center of our interior life, we seek to be with Jesus among God and men." The Conciliar decree *Presbyterorum Ordinis* affirmed: "The Lord Jesus . . . makes his whole Mystical Body sharer in the anointing of the Spirit wherewith he has been anointed: for in that Body all the faithful are made a holy and kingly priesthood, they offer spiritual sacrifices to God through Jesus Christ, and they proclaim the virtues of him who has called them out of darkness into his admirable light. Therefore there is no such thing as a member that has not a share in the mission of the whole Body. Rather, every single member ought to reverence Jesus in his heart and by the spirit of prophecy give testimony of Jesus" (no. 2).

This implies that all the faithful are directly committed to apostolate by virtue of their consecration at baptism. This was affirmed by the decree *Apostolicam Actuositatem,* ". . . the Church exercises it [apostolate] through all its members, though in various ways. In fact, the Christian vocation is, of its nature, a vocation to the apostolate as well" (no. 2). This truth was clearly the lifeblood of Opus Dei from the moment of its foundation, but written evidence is found in a text written by Saint Josemaría in 1932: "The prejudice that ordinary faithful can do no more than limit themselves to assisting the clergy in ecclesiastical apostolates must be rejected. There is no reason why the apostolate of the laity always has to be simply a participation in the apostolate of the hierarchy: they have the duty of doing apostolate. And this not because they receive a canonical mission, but because they are part of the Church. They carry out . . . this mission through their profession, trade, family, relations with colleagues, and friendships."

If one wanted to describe what the founder did during the council, one might say: a lot of prayer and penance so that the Holy Spirit guide those assembled and the Church. And he urged all his sons and daughters to do likewise.

During the period of the council, in November, 1965, Paul VI inaugurated the *Centro ELIS* in the Tiburtino neighborhood of Rome, in the presence of thousands of people, many Council participants and Monsignor Escrivá. Centro ELIS is a center for the education of working youth in a neighborhood on the outskirts of Rome, which at that time was rather run-down. Blessed John XXIII had originally entrusted the task to Opus Dei. Pope Paul, seeing this living demonstration of faith, exclaimed,

"Tutto qui è Opus Dei" (Everything here is the Work of God).

Saint Josemaría later confided:

"I was deeply moved. I've always been deeply moved: with Pius XII, with John XXIII and with Paul VI, because I have faith."

November 21, 1967, Pope Paul VI inaugurates Centro ELIS, in Rome.

Holiness and the Council

"We should not be surprised therefore that the Second Vatican Council, when teaching on the mystery of the Church, placed special emphasis on this most important mark of holiness, to which the others are intimately united, and has repeatedly invited all Christians of every condition and social class to the fullness of Christian life and the perfection of charity. This call to holiness is considered the most characteristic element of the entire teaching of the Council and, as it were, its ultimate purpose" (Paul VI, Motu proprio Sanctitas Clarior, *March 19, 1969*).

DIFFICULT TIMES

On December 22, 1971, a beautiful antique image of the Blessed Mother arrived at Villa Tevere. It was a wooden sculpture, almost life-size and . . . badly in need of restoration. It was a gift to the founder from his Italian sons and daughters. Seeing it, Saint Josemaría addressed our Lady with words of affection while asking from what Church it had been removed. He had it restored as quickly as possible and asked that in the meantime it be mounted in an appropriate temporary site, with freshly cut flowers always kept at our Lady's feet. He wanted to make reparation in this way for all the images that had been removed from churches, for the confessionals eliminated, the Eucharist neglected, dogmas attacked, obedience derided, and piety drained.

Those were difficult times. After the council there were many arbitrary and questionable interpretations of its texts, people justifying their claims by appeal to the so-called "spirit of the council."

The founder had the habit of inscribing a sentence on the first page of his liturgical calendar, as a motto for the entire year. On New Year's Day of 1970 he wrote: *Beata Maria intercedente, fortes in fide!* ("Through the intercession of Blessed Mary, may we be strong in the Faith"). But inside he was heartbroken. An alarmed Paul VI denounced signs of the "decomposition of the Church" and the "smoke of Satan" that was penetrating into it. Although he did not want to sadden his followers, he sometimes confided in them: "I am suffering very much, my children. We are living in a time of madness. Millions of souls are confused. There is great danger that, in practice, the Sacraments will be emptied of their content—all of them, including even Baptism—and that the very commandments of God's law will lose their meaning for consciences.

Afterwards he consoled them, "You know very well that the Church will not die, because our Lord promised that it would not, and his word is infallible. Nonetheless, I have to say that things are going very badly, and I would not be a good pastor if I didn't tell you. . . . Many times I prefer to keep you from suffering and bear the pain alone."

"A flock is in good shape," he also said, "when the shepherds are concerned for the sheep; when they loose the dogs on the wolf; when they do not bring the flock to graze in areas where the grass is poisonous, but where they can find nourishing foliage. The same thing happens with souls. We need shepherds who are not mute sheepdogs, because the dogs, if they remain silent, are useless: they should be barking to sound the alarm." Viewing the rebellion which confronted the Holy Father, he said, "Pray much for the current Pope and for the Pope who is to come, who will have to be a martyr from the very first day." He wrote a long letter to all his children urging them "to defend from any possible attack the authority of the Roman Pontiff, which cannot be limited by anyone except God."

A time to pray. That's how he defined it. Those years were more than ever a time for prayer. And suffering. In 1970 he had thousands of rosary beads purchased, and gave them out to whoever came to see him, asking them to pray for the Church. It was a time to turn to the Mother of the Church so that the "time of trial" would be cut short. He went forth on a series of Marian pilgrimages, the sorrow in his heart mitigated only by a robust supernatural hope and his instinctive good humor.

November, 1972, Saint Josemaría at Fatima.

"I am going to visit two shrines of the Blessed Virgin," he wrote to his children prior to a trip to the Iberian Peninsula. "I am going like a pilgrim of the twelfth century: with the same love, with the same simplicity, with the same joy. I will pray there for the world, for the Church, for the Pope and for the Work. . . . Join me in my prayers and in my Mass." In April of 1970 he went to Fatima and Torreciudad, the mountain chapel to which he was brought after his cure in 1904 and where through his efforts work on a large shrine had just commenced.

Added to his concern for the Church was his preoccupation with the definitive juridical status of Opus Dei. The figure of secular institute had already appeared inadequate to the founder from the moment of the first pontifical approval in 1947, but it had to be accepted until such time as a canonical framework suitable for the theological and pastoral phenomenon of Opus Dei could be found. New possibilities were opened by Vatican II that would later be developed in canon law—specifically, the provision for personal prelatures.

Praying at the Shrine of our Lady of Lujan, in Argentina.

In this spirit of concern he traveled to the shrine of Guadalupe, in Mexico, in May, 1970. He made a novena to our Lady there, praying for the Church and for the Work. Kneeling in a small balcony facing the sanctuary, he recited the Rosary and spoke aloud to Mary with moving childlike trust. "Lady, I bring you—for I have nothing else—thorns, the ones I have in my heart. But I am sure that with you they will turn to roses . . . Grant that we may have in us, in our hearts, little roses blooming all the year round: the roses of daily life, ordinary roses, but filled with the perfume of sacrifice and love. I have said little roses, on purpose, because it suits me better, for in my whole life I have only been able to do ordinary, everyday things, and even then I often haven't been able to finish them. But I am sure that it is there, in my everyday ordinary behavior, that you and your Son are waiting for me."

At another point he continued, "Here I am. Because you can do everything! Because you love! My mother, our Mother . . . , keep us from everything that stops us being your children, everything that is trying to obstruct our path and spoil our vocation. . . . Hail Mary, Daughter of God the Father; Hail Mary, Mother of God the Son; Hail Mary, Spouse of God the Holy Spirit; Hail Mary, Temple of the Most Holy Trinity: greater than you, no one but God! Show us that you are our Mother! Show what you are able to bring about!"

To console the Pope, Saint Josemaría requested an audience and was received on June 25, 1973. He did not go to ask for anything, only to give the Holy Father a bit of good news: the fidelity of thousands of persons in the Work, the ordination of a good number of professionals to be priests, 100 percent priests, the blossoming apostolate in so many parts of the world. Paul VI understood, and he was grateful.

Shrine of our Lady of Guadalupe, Mexico, 1970.

A "traveling contemplative"

"The salient features of his personality are to be found not only in his extraordinary talents as a man of action, but above all in the life of prayer and constant union with God that made him a 'traveling contemplative.' Faithful to the gifts he had received, he gave an example of heroism in the most ordinary situations, in a life of constant prayer, in uninterrupted mortifications which were 'like the beating of the heart,' in assiduous presence of God that could attain to the heights of union amid the hustle and bustle of daily life, and in intense persevering work" (Decree on the Heroicity of Virtues, April 9, 1990).

CATECHETICAL TRIPS

Starting in 1970, the founder of Opus Dei decided to undertake catechetical trips to various countries. With doubt and uncertainty spreading among the faithful, it was time to put his shoulder to the wheel, to proclaim the authentic teachings of the Church to large numbers of people and thus strengthen their faith. The method that he liked to use was one of personal contact, and personal it was for each of those present, despite the numbers that came to listen to him. Questions and answers, jokes and prayer, stories, and truths proclaimed loudly and firmly.

He began in 1970 in Mexico, in conjunction with his pilgrimage to Guadalupe. He met with groups from different walks of life. Among them some country-

With a group of Mexican campesinos.

folk from Morelos, where members of Opus Dei, together with other people, had started a farm school. To them he said, "All of us, you and we, are concerned with improving things for you, so you can get out of this situation, so that you are not under financial burdens . . . We are also going to do our best so that your children acquire culture. You'll see how between us all we will succeed, and so those who are talented and want to study, can rise high. At first they won't be many, but as the years go by . . . And how will we do it? As if we were doing a favor? . . . No, my children, not that way! Haven't I just told you we are all equal?"

In 1972 he set aside time for a two-month swing through a string of cities in Spain and Portugal, filling his schedule with all types of meetings, many of which were filmed. It was an exhausting journey, though one would not guess it from the drive and animation shown by the founder in those films. To a veritable kaleidoscope of questions submitted, he responded with style and understanding, with the simplicity of a catechist but with the doctrine of a theologian and the faith of a saint. People asked him questions about the sacraments, about devotion to our Lady, about prayer, about family life—questions, for the most part, that had been widely debated, leaving a trail of perplexity in the souls of the faithful.

"In the get-togethers that the apostles had with our Lord, they talked about everything: *in multis argumentis,* as Sacred Scripture says. Our get-togethers have that evangelical feel to them: they are a friendly way of speaking in family about the teaching of Jesus Christ. You see I am not exaggerating when I tell you that Opus Dei is a great catechesis."

He encouraged people to ask "impertinent" questions, and a few took him at his word.

"Father, how do you spend the time of thanksgiving after Communion?"

"This fellow wants me to confess in public!"

But he did answer, speaking of his effort to prolong the thanksgiving until noon, and then to begin preparing for the next day's Mass. The one who asked had received a thought-provoking suggestion.

"Father, what virtues do you think are most important in a teacher?"

"You need them all, but above all show the students a lot of loyalty."

"Father, how can we help friends recover the faith they claim to have lost?"

"If they truly had the faith, it may be that they have not really lost it. It can happen that over the faith right now there is a shell, and another on top of

An encounter during the 1974 trips of catechesis.

that, and another: a series of layers of indifference, of misguided readings, perhaps of bad habits, and bad influences. I counsel you first and foremost to pray."

"Father, some say that we should teach all the religions to children so that they can choose among them when they are older . . . "

And so on and so forth with questions and answers of surprising spontaneity. His preaching in those weeks reached more than 150,000 people. In every city he wanted to visit cloistered convents to show his love for the religious vocation and ask for prayers. He also made a pilgrimage to the most important shrine of our Lady in each place he visited.

Between May and August of 1974 he traveled through South America: Brazil, Argentina, Chile, Peru, Ecuador, and Venezuela. Once again he wanted to strengthen the souls of the faithful in their love for the Church and the Pope, and in their fidelity to the Magisterium. The gatherings on each leg of the trip were numerous and well attended, as the films illustrate. In Peru a nasty bronchitis confined him to bed, and the doctors expressed their worries. While not completely recovered, he started preaching again. On the first of August in Ecuador a bad case of *el soroche* (altitude sickness) gripped him with unusual violence, and the doctors prescribed a suspension of all activity. But he plowed ahead, there and later in Venezuela, and took part in at least some get-togethers, even though he was running a high fever.

In February of 1975 he returned to the Western Hemisphere, visiting Venezuela and Guatemala. On this last leg of the trip he fell ill again; left without any energy whatsoever, he had to cut the trip short.

In all of these get-togethers, he dwelt on the necessity of conversion, emphasizing frequent recourse to sacramental confession. He said that if even one person was inspired to go to confession, he would consider the time of his trip well spent.

On a journey, in 1975.

Love for the Church

"'And, apart from other things, there is the daily pressure upon me of my anxiety for all the churches,' Saint Paul wrote. This sigh of the Apostle is a reminder for all Christians—for you, too—of our duty to place at the feet of the Spouse of Christ, of the Holy Church, all that we are and all that we can be; loving her faithfully, even at the cost of livelihood, of honor, of life itself" (The Forge, 584).

I SEEK YOUR FACE

On March 28, 1975, Father Josemaría completed fifty years of priesthood. He did not want any festivities, he wished to spend that day—which fell on Good Friday—in recollection and prayer, continuing to live the "hide and disappear" that he had adopted as a rule of life in order to give all glory to Jesus Christ. On the eve of the anniversary he made his prayer aloud, opening his heart to God and to those sons of his with him in the chapel.

"Fifty years have gone by, and I am still like a babbling child. I am just beginning, beginning again, as I do each day in my interior life. And it will be so to the end of my days . . . A glance backwards . . . What an immense panorama, so many sorrows, so many joys. But now all is joy, all joy . . . because experience teaches us that sorrow is the chiseling of

the divine artist, who is eager to make of each one of us, of this shapeless mass that we are, a crucifix, a Christ, that *alter Christus* each one of us is called to be.

"My Lord, thank you for everything. Many thanks! . . . I have habitually given you thanks . . . And now many lips, many hearts, are together repeating the same cry to you: *gratias tibi, Deus, gratias tibi!*, for we have motives only for giving thanks.

"We should never be afraid of anything. We must never let anything worry us. We must never lose our peace of mind over anything whatsoever. . . . Lord, grant my children peace of mind. Don't let them lose it even if they commit a serious error. If they realize that they've done wrong, that in itself is already a grace, a light from heaven.

"*Gratias tibi, Deus, gratias tibi!* The life of each one of us ought to be a hymn of thanksgiving; just look how Opus Dei has come about. You, Lord, have done it all, with a handful of good-for-nothings . . . *Stulta mundi, infirma mundi, et ea quae non sunt.* Saint Paul's teaching has been fulfilled to the letter. You have laid hold of instruments that were utterly illogical and in no way suitable, and you have spread the Work all over the world. People are thanking you all over Europe, and in places in Asia and Africa, and in the whole of America, and in Australia. Everywhere they are giving you thanks."

By then his eyesight had deteriorated significantly, but he adjusted to this with such naturalness that only the persons closest to him were aware of it. He took to saying once again the aspiration of his youth, *Domine, ut videam!,* but infusing it with an entirely new depth of meaning. On March 19 he poured out his soul to his Jesus: "Lord, I can do no more, and yet I have to be strong for my children's sake. I can't see three meters ahead and I have to peer into the future, to point out the way for my children. You, help me: let me see with your eyes, my Christ, Jesus my Love!"

In the month of May, the founder of Opus Dei made his last trip, visiting the shrine of Torreciudad, by then almost finished. He became completely absorbed in contemplating the reredos, a large altar

Saint Josemaría contemplates the altarpiece, Shrine of our Lady of Torreciudad.

sculpture with scenes of the life of Mary, and in the center, from top to bottom, the tabernacle, the crucifixion, and the ancient venerated image of our Lady of Torreciudad. In these months he frequently repeated the aspiration "I seek your face." "Lord I have a great wish to see you face to face, to admire your countenance, to contemplate you! . . . I love you so much, desire so much to see you, Lord!"

On June 26, 1975, he got up early, as usual,

made the usual half hour of prayer and celebrated Mass about 8 o'clock. After a quick breakfast he asked those who were with him to tell a particular person that: "For years I have been offering the Holy Mass for the Church and particularly for the Holy Father. . . . This very day I have offered my life to our Lord for the Pope. . . ."

About 9:30 am they left for Castelgandolfo where they would get together in a family-style formative meeting with his daughters at the Roman College of Saint Mary. It was a very hot day. During the ride they prayed the Rosary and conversed pleasantly.

"You have priestly souls," he said to those young women upon his arrival. "I will repeat it as I do every time I come here. . . . Your brothers who are not priests also have priestly souls. With this priestly soul you can and should help out, and with God's grace, along with the priestly ministry of the priests of the Work, we shall work effectively. . . . I suppose that in everything you do . . . you find a reason to talk to God and to his Blessed Mother, who is our Mother, and to St. Joseph, our father and lord, and to our Guardian Angels so as to help this Holy Church, our Mother, who is in such great need, and who is having such a difficult time in the world these days. We should love the Church very much and the Pope, whoever he may be. Ask our Lord that our service on behalf of the Church and the Pope may be effective."

After twenty minutes or so he felt ill. He returned to Rome with Fr. Álvaro del Portillo and Fr. Javier Echevarría. Back at Villa Tevere, they greeted our Lord in the tabernacle, and then went toward the room where he worked. Having just crossed its threshold, he glanced lovingly at the image of our Lady, and said to Fr. Javier:

"Javi! . . . I don't feel well."

He collapsed on the floor.

During his stay in Mexico, in 1970, he had contemplated an image of our Lady of Guadalupe handing a rose to the Indian Juan Diego. He said that he would like to die like that, looking at the Blessed Mother while she offered him a flower. It was the image of our Lady of Guadalupe, presiding over his office in Villa Tevere, that received his last glance on earth.

The image on which his last glance rested. At the right, he celebrates Mass.

I WILL HELP YOU MORE

His body, clothed with priestly vestments, was placed at the foot of the altar in Santa Maria della Pace (today the Church of the Prelature). His sons and daughters followed one another keeping an uninterrupted vigil next to his body. In their sorrow, they recalled what he had often repeated in his last years:

"I am not necessary. I will help you more from heaven. You will know how to do things better than me. I am not necessary." The news of his death raced through Rome and echoed around the world. A constant stream of mourners poured into Villa Tevere. The face of Saint Josemaría emanated an ineffable peace. Cardinals and bishops were among those paying their respects.

The funeral in Rome and the requiem Masses all over world were a singular moment of sorrow, joy, and conversion. It was the death of a father and a saint.

A reputation for holiness had already characterized him during his lifetime, from the first years of his priestly ministry. Alongside him one could feel God's presence. His entire person spoke of God.

Spending time with him one felt drawn toward our Lord. Even in those crowded gatherings he managed not to be the center of attention, even though ostensibly he was, by turning hearts toward Jesus Christ. Thousands who attended his Masses were moved by the thought:

"Here is a priest in love with God!"

Many priests and seminarians who attended the retreats he preached all over Spain between 1938 and 1945 had lifelong memories of the ardent fire of the love of God transmitted by "that holy priest." Leopoldo Eijo y Garay, the bishop of Madrid who in the first years of Opus Dei understood its spirit and protected Saint Josemaría, was known to comment, "I hope that this will be my credentials when I face the judgment of God."

The people who knew him in the early years spoke to others, testifying to their conviction of his singular holiness of life. From the time he settled in Rome in 1946, people from all over the world came to see him, to listen to his words, confident that God would speak to them through him. People commended all sorts of intentions to him, and were reassured when he promised to remember some-

May 17, 1992, during the beatification of Josemaría Escrivá and Josephine Bakhita.

thing in his Mass. On the rare occasions in which it was possible, the people thronged about him to listen, to kiss his hand, or ask him to bless religious objects that they then kept as relics.

This reputation grew with the passage of time, as the last catechetical trips illustrate. Even while speaking always of God, Saint Josemaría immediately created a family atmosphere based on simplicity and trust. And devotion to him spread quickly after his death, as shown by the crowds that gathered

every year at the Anniversary Masses said in suffrage in cities around the world, as well as the constant pilgrimages to his tomb, in the crypt of Our Lady of Peace, in Villa Tevere.

From 1975 on, continuous news of favors received through his intercession poured in from around the world. They ran the gamut from assistance in daily problems to true miracles, including inexplicable cures, solutions to family problems, work-related favors . . . Particularly numerous were spiritual favors: radical conversions as well as developing closer ties with our Lord.

These had always been the graces most dear to his heart. When the shrine of Torreciudad was under construction, for example, he assured others that in that place would come "a shower of spiritual favors . . . which our Lord will want to do for those who invoke his Blessed Mother . . . That is why I want many confessionals there, where people can be cleansed in the holy sacrament of penance and—their souls renewed— can confirm or renew their lives as Christians, learn to sanctify and love their work, and bring the peace and joy of Jesus Christ to their homes . . ."

Sixty-nine cardinals, and approximately 1300 bishops from all over the world, 41 superiors of religious congregations, priests, religious, representatives of lay associations, civil authorities and thousands of others asked the Holy Father to open the cause of beatification and canonization, manifesting their own conviction that this would be a great good for the Church.

On February 19, 1981 Cardinal Ugo Poletti promulgated the decree that introduced the cause. On November 8, 1986 the evidentiary phase on the life and virtues of the Servant of God Josemaría Escrivá was completed. A parallel process conducted by the archdiocese of Madrid had concluded on June 26, 1984. On April 9, 1990, the Holy Father John Paul II declared the heroicity of the virtues of the Servant of God Josemaría Escrivá. On July 6, 1991, in the presence of the Holy Father, the decree sanctioning the miraculous character of a cure worked through the intercession of the founder of Opus Dei was read. This concluded the steps needed for beatification.

On May 17, 1992, a great crowd filled St. Peter's Square, spilling over into the square of Pius XII and the Via della Conciliazione. Perched on the loggias of St. Peter's Basilica were large portraits of Josemaría Escrivá and Sister Josephine Bakhita, the two persons proclaimed Blessed by John Paul II.

Beatification of Josemaría Escrivá. Pope John Paul II and Bishop Alvaro del Portillo.

A pontifical decree of December 20, 2001, recognized the miraculous character of a second cure attributed to Blessed Josemaría's intercession. This opened the door to his canonization, which was then scheduled by John Paul II for October 6, 2002.

A joyful son

"The spiritual and apostolic life of the newly Blessed was based on knowing himself, through faith, to be a son of God in Christ. This faith nourished his love for the Lord, his evangelizing drive, his constant joy, even in the great trials and difficulties he had to overcome" (John Paul II, "Homily at the Beatification," May 17, 1992).

Inside the Gospel
As One more Character

"We have to learn from him, from Jesus who is our only model. If you want to go forward without stumbling or wandering off the path, then all you have to do is walk the road he walked, placing your feet in his footprints and entering into his humble and patient Heart, there to drink from the well-springs of his commandments and of his love. In a word, you must identify yourself with Jesus Christ and try to become really and truly another Christ among your fellow men."[1]

Identification with Christ was the point of all the formation Saint Josemaría transmitted, the point of departure and the point of arrival. Christ is Love with a capital "L", he is everything. That is all the more reason why we need to get to know him well, to live our ordinary lives together with him, and to live *his* historical life together with *him*: in other words, to enter into the Gospels.

"If you wish to get close to our Lord through the pages of the Gospels, I always recommend that you try to enter into the scene by taking part as just one more person there. In this way (and I know many perfectly ordinary people who live this way) you will be captivated as Mary was, who hung on every word that Jesus uttered or, like Martha, you will boldly make your worries known to him, opening your heart sincerely about them no matter how little they may be."[2]

The following commentaries on Gospel scenes evoke mysteries of the life of Jesus. All are taken from the works of Saint Josemaría. While they do not pretend to be exhaustive nor even schematic, they do suggest the type of meditation on the Gospel that he encouraged.

Ecce Homo,
Juan de Juanes
(c. 1510–1579),
Madrid, Prado
Museum.

[1] *Friends of God*, 128.
[2] *Friends of God*, 222.

THE ANNUNCIATION

"In the sixth month the angel Gabriel was sent from God to a city of Galilee named Nazareth, to a virgin betrothed to a man whose name was Joseph, of the house of David; and the virgin's name was Mary" (Lk1:26–27).

"Don't forget, my friend, that we are children. The Lady of the sweet name, Mary, is withdrawn in prayer. You, in that house, are whatever you want to be: a friend, a servant, an onlooker, a neighbor ... —I, at this moment, don't dare to be anything. I hide behind you; full of awe, I contemplate the scene: The Archangel delivers his message . . . *Quomodo fiet istud, quoniam virum non cognosco?* —How shall this be done since I know not man? (*Lk* 1:34).

"Our Mother's voice brings to my memory—by contrast—all the impurities of men . . . . mine too. And then how I hate the low, mean things of the earth ... What resolutions!"[3]

"Our mother is a model of correspondence to grace. If we contemplate her life, our Lord will give us the light we need to divinize our everyday existence. . . . First, let us imitate her love. Charity cannot be content with just nice feelings; it must find its way into our conversations and, above all, into our deeds. The Virgin did not merely pronounce her *fiat;*

The Annunciation,
*Martin Schongauer
(c. 1445–1491),
Colmar, Unterlinden
Museum.*

in every moment she fulfilled that firm and irrevocable decision. So should we. When God's love gets through to us and we come to know what he desires, we ought to commit ourselves to be faithful, loyal—and then be so in fact. Because 'not everyone who says to me, Lord, Lord, will enter the kingdom of heaven, but he who does the will of my Father in heaven' (*Mt* 7:21).

"We must imitate her natural and supernatural refinement. She is a privileged creature in the history of salvation, for in Mary 'the Word became flesh and dwelled among us' (*Jn* 1:14). But she is a reserved, quiet witness. She never wished to be praised, for she never sought her own glory. Mary is present at the mysteries surrounding the infancy of her Son, but these are 'normal' mysteries, so to speak. When the great miracles take place and the crowds acclaim them in amazement, she is nowhere to be found. In Jerusalem when Christ, riding a little donkey, is proclaimed king, we don't catch a glimpse of Mary. But after all have fled, she reappears next to the cross. This way of acting bespeaks personal greatness and depth, the sanctity of her soul.

"Following her example of obedience to God, we can learn to serve delicately without being slavish. In Mary we don't find the slightest trace of the attitude of the foolish virgins, who obey, but thoughtlessly. Our Lady listens attentively to what God wants, ponders what she doesn't fully understand and asks about what she doesn't know. Then she gives herself completely to doing God's will: 'Behold the handmaid of the Lord, be it done unto me according to your word.' Isn't that marvelous? The Blessed Virgin, our teacher in all we do, shows us here that obedience to God is not servile, does not bypass our conscience. We should be inwardly moved to discover 'the freedom of the children of God.'"[4]

[3] *Holy Rosary,* first joyful mystery.
[4] *Christ Is Passing By,* 173.

THE BIRTH OF OUR LORD

"And while they were there, the time came for her to be delivered. And she gave birth to her first-born son and wrapped him in swaddling clothes and laid him in a manger, because there was no place for them in the inn" (Lk 2:6–7).

"A decree of Caesar Augustus has been proclaimed, ordering the whole world to be enrolled. For this purpose, every person must go to the city of his ancestors. —Since Joseph is of the house and family of David, he goes with the Virgin Mary from Nazareth to the city called Bethlehem, in Judea.

"And in Bethlehem is born our God: Jesus Christ! —There is no room at the inn: He is born in a stable. —And His Mother wraps Him in swaddling clothes and lays Him in a manger.

"Cold. —Poverty . . . —I am Joseph's little servant. —How good Joseph is! —He treats me like a father. —He even forgives me if I take the Child in my arms and spend hour after hour saying sweet and loving things to Him! . . .

"And I kiss Him —you kiss Him too! —and I rock Him in my arms, and I sing to Him, and I call Him King, Love, my God, my Only-one, my All! . . ."[5]

"And in that region there were shepherds out in the field, keeping watch over their flock by night. And an angel of the Lord appeared to them and the glory of the Lord shone around them, and they were filled with fear. And the angel said to them, 'Be not afraid; for behold, I bring you good news of a great joy which will come to all the people; for to you is born this day in the city of David a savior, who is Christ the Lord. And this will be a sign for you: you will find a babe wrapped in swaddling clothes and lying in a manger.' And suddenly there was with the angel a multitude of the heavenly host praising God and saying, 'Glory to God in the highest, and on earth peace among men of good will!'" (Lk 2:8–14)

"*Jesus Christus, Deus homo*: Jesus Christ, God-man. This is one of 'the mighty works of God,' which we should reflect upon and thank him for. He has come to bring 'peace on earth to men of good will,' to all men who want to unite their wills to the holy will of God—not just the rich, not just the poor, but everyone: all the brethren. We are all brothers in Jesus, children of God, brothers and sisters of Christ. His Mother is our mother.

"There is only one race in the world: the race of the children of God. We should all speak the same language, taught us by our Father in heaven—the language Jesus spoke with his Father. It is the language of heart and mind, which you are using now, in your prayer—the language of contemplation, used by people who are spiritual, because they realize they are children of God. This language is expressed in a thousand motions of our will, in the clear insights of our minds, in the affections of our heart, in our commitment to lead a virtuous life, in goodness, happiness and peace.

"You must look at the Child in the manger. He is our Love. Look at him, realizing that the whole thing is a mystery. We need to accept this mystery on faith and use our faith to explore it very deeply. To do this, we must have the humble attitude of a Christian soul. Let us not try to reduce the greatness of God to our own poor ideas and human explanations. Let us try to understand that this mystery, for all its darkness, is a light to guide men's lives."[6]

The Birth of Christ, Johyann Koerbecke (1446–1491), Nuremberg, National Museum.

[5] *Holy Rosary*, third joyful mystery
[6] *Christ Is Passing By,* 13.

IN THE HOUSE AT NAZARETH

"And he went down with them and came to Nazareth, and was obedient to them; and his mother kept all these things in her heart. And Jesus increased in wisdom and in stature, and in favor with God and man" (Lk 2:51–52).

"The fact that Jesus grew up and lived just like us shows us that human existence, people's ordinary everyday activity, has a divine meaning. No matter how much we may have reflected on all this, we should always be surprised when we think of the thirty years of obscurity which made up the greater part of Jesus' life among us. He lived in obscurity, but, for us, that period is full of light. It illuminates our days and fills them with meaning, for we are ordinary Christians who lead an ordinary life, just like millions of other people all over the world.

"That was the way Jesus lived for thirty years, as 'the son of the carpenter.' There followed three years of public life, spent among the crowds. People were surprised: 'Who is this?' they asked. 'Where has he learned these things?' For he was just like them: he had shared the life of ordinary people. He was 'the carpenter, the son of Mary.' And he was God; he was achieving the redemption of mankind and 'drawing all things to himself.'"[7]

Saint Josemaría Escrivá felt compelled by God's call to imitate the "hidden" life of Jesus in a special way, the ordinary life so similar to the daily occupations of most people. In his teachings he promoted this ideal.

"I dream—and the dream has come true—of multitudes of God's children, sanctifying themselves as ordinary citizens, sharing the ambitions and en-

The Holy Family, Jan Sons (1547/8–1611/4), Parma, Madonna della Steccata.

deavors of their colleagues and friends. I want to shout aloud to them this divine truth: if you are there in the middle of ordinary life, it doesn't mean Christ has forgotten about you or hasn't called you. He has invited you to stay among the activities and concerns of the world. He wants you to know that your human vocation, your profession, your talents, are not outside his divine plans. He has sanctified them and made them a most pleasing offering to his Father."[8]

Another theme that was never absent in his reflection on the years at Nazareth was that of St. Joseph. His devotion to the holy patriarch would grow impetuously right up to the end of his life. Here are a few excerpts from his homily on St. Joseph in *Christ Is Passing By*:

"But if Joseph learned from Jesus to live in a divine way, I would be bold enough to say that, humanly speaking, there was much he taught God's Son. There is something I do not quite like in that title of foster father which is sometimes given to Joseph, because it might make us think of the relationship between Joseph and Jesus as something cold and external. Certainly our faith tells us that he was not his father according to the flesh, but this is not the only kind of fatherhood. . . .

"Joseph loved Jesus as a father loves his son and showed his love by giving him the best he had. Joseph, caring for the child as he had been commanded, made Jesus a craftsman, transmitting his own professional skill to him. So the neighbors of Nazareth will call Jesus both *faber* and *fabri filius*: the craftsman and the son of the craftsman. Jesus worked in Joseph's workshop and by Joseph's side. What must Joseph have been, how grace must have worked through him, that he should be able to fulfill this task of the human upbringing of the Son of God!

"For Jesus must have resembled Joseph: in his way of working, in the features of his character, in his way of speaking. Jesus' realism, his eye for detail, the way he sat at table and broke bread, his preference for using everyday situations to give doctrine—all this reflects his childhood and the influence of Joseph."[9]

[7] *Christ Is Passing By*, 14
[8] *Christ Is Passing By*, 20.
[9] *Christ Is Passing By*, 55.

TEMPTATIONS IN THE DESERT

The Temptations of Christ, Beato Angelico (1387–1455), Florence, Museum of San Marco.

"Then Jesus was led by the Spirit into the wilderness to be tempted by the devil. And he fasted forty days and forty nights, and afterwards he was hungry. And the tempter came and said to him, 'If you are the Son of God, command these stones to become loaves of bread.'

But he answered, 'It is written: Man shall not live by bread alone, but by every word that proceeds from the mouth of God'" (Mt 4:1–4).

"The whole episode is a mystery which man cannot hope to understand: God submitting to temptation, letting the evil one have his way. But we can meditate upon it, asking our Lord to help us understand the teaching it contains.

"Jesus Christ being tempted . . . Tradition likes to see Christ's trials in this way: our Lord, who came to be an example to us in all things, wants to suffer temptation as well. And so it happens, for Christ was perfect man, like us in everything except sin. After forty days of fasting, with perhaps no food other than herbs and roots and a little water, he feels hungry—he is really hungry, as anyone would be. And when the devil suggests he turn stones into bread, our Lord not only declines the food which his body requires, but he also rejects a greater temptation: that of using his divine power to solve, if we can express it so, a personal problem.

"You have noticed how, throughout the Gospels, Jesus doesn't work miracles for his own benefit. He turns water into wine for the wedding guests at Cana; he multiplies loaves and fish for the hungry crowd. But he earns his bread, for years, with his own work. And later, during his journeys through the land of Israel, he lives with the help of those who follow him.

"Saint John tells how after a long journey when Jesus arrived at the well of Sichar, he sent his disciples into town to buy food. And when he sees the Samaritan woman coming, he asks her for water, since he has no way of getting it. His body, worn out from a long journey, feels weary. On other occasions he has to yield to sleep to regain his strength. How generous our Lord is in humbling himself and fully accepting his human condition! He does not use his divine power to escape from difficulties or effort. Let's pray that he will teach us to be tough, to love work, to appreciate the human and divine nobility of savoring the consequences of self-giving."[10]

"In the hour of temptation, practice the virtue of Hope, saying: For my rest and enjoyment I have the whole of eternity ahead of me. Here and now, full of Faith, I will earn my rest through work and win my joy through suffering. What will Love be like in Heaven!

"Better still, you should practice your Love by saying: What I want is to please my God, my Love, by doing his Will in all things, as though there were neither reward nor punishment—simply to please him."[11]

---

[10] *Christ Is Passing By,* 61.
[11] *The Forge,* 1008.

CALLING THE APOSTLES

"In these days he went out into the hills to pray; and all night he continued in prayer to God. And when it was day, he called his disciples, and chose from them twelve, whom he named apostles; Simon, whom he named Peter, and Andrew his brother, and James and John, and Philip, and Bartholomew, and Matthew, and Thomas, and James the son of Alphaeus, and Simon who was called the Zealot, and Judas the son of James, and Judas Iscariot, who became a traitor" (Lk 6:12–16).

"I'm greatly encouraged whenever I consider a written precedent for what we have been talking about. We find it, step by step, in the Gospel's account of the vocation of the first twelve. Let's meditate on it slowly, asking those holy witnesses of our Lord to help us follow Christ as they did.

"The first apostles, for whom I have great affection and devotion, were nothing to boast about, humanly speaking. With the exception of Matthew, who probably earned a comfortable living which he left behind at the behest of Jesus, the apostles were mere fishermen. They lived a meager existence, fishing all night to keep food on the table.

"But social status is unimportant. They weren't

educated; they weren't even very bright, if we judge from their reaction to supernatural things. Finding even the most elementary examples and comparisons beyond their reach, they would turn to the Master and ask: 'Explain the parable to us.' When Jesus uses the image of the 'leaven' of the Pharisees, they think that he's reproaching them for not having purchased bread.

"They were poor; they were ignorant. They weren't very simple or open. But they were even ambitious. Frequently they argued over who would be the greatest when—according to their understanding —Christ would definitively restore the kingdom of Israel. Amid the intimacy of the last supper, during that sublime moment when Jesus is about to immolate himself for all of humanity, we find them arguing heatedly.

"Faith? They had little. Jesus Christ himself points this out. They had seen the dead raised, all kinds of sicknesses cured, bread and fish multiplied, storms calmed, devils cast out. Chosen as the head, Saint Peter is the only one who reacts quickly: 'You are the Christ, the Son of the living God.' But it is a faith beset by limitations, which led Peter to reproach Jesus Christ for his desire to suffer and die for the redemption of men. And Jesus had to upbraid him: 'Get behind me, Satan! You are a hindrance to me; for you are not on the side of God, but of men.'. . .

". . . And did these men of little faith at least stand out in their love for Christ? Undoubtedly they loved him, at least in word. At times they were swept away by enthusiasm: 'Let us also go, that we may die with him.' But at the moment of truth, they all fled, except for John who truly loved with deeds. Only this adolescent, youngest of the apostles, can be found next to the cross. The others didn't find within themselves that love as strong as death.

"These were the disciples called by our Lord. Such stuff is what Christ chose. And they remain just like that until they are filled with the Holy Spirit and thus become pillars of the Church(cf. Gal 2:9). They are ordinary men, complete with defects and shortcomings, more eager to say than to do. Nevertheless, Jesus calls them to be fishers of men (Mt 4:19), coredeemers, dispensers of the grace of God.

"Something similar has happened to us . . ."[12]

Christ among the Apostles, *Milan, San Lorenzo Maggiore.*

[12] *Christ Is Passing By*, 2–3.

CONVERSING WITH EVERYONE

"All this Jesus said to the crowds in parables"
(*Mt* 13:34).

"Our Lord does not limit his dialogue to a small, restricted group: he talks with everyone. With the holy women, with the entire crowd; with representatives of the upper classes of Israel like Nicodemus, and with publicans like Zacchaeus; with scrupulously observant persons, and with sinners like the Samaritan woman; with the sick and with the healthy; with the poor, whom he loved with all his heart; with the doctors of the law and with pagans, whose faith he praised as greater than any in Israel; with the elderly and with children.

"Jesus does not deny anyone his word, and it is a word which heals, which consoles, which enlightens. How many times I have meditated and had others meditate upon this apostolic style of Christ, at once both human and divine, based on friendship and confidence!

"Recall Christ's conversation with the Samaritan woman. What a marvelous way of speaking! He knows how to say things in such a way that this woman is transformed from a sinner to a proclaimer of the truth: 'Come, see a man who told me all that I ever did. Can this be the Christ?' They went out of the city and were coming to him. Yes, my daughters and sons, the dialogue of Christ is not a will-o'–the-wisp, nor a vain mental exercise; it is the word of truth that ignites and enkindles with a divine flame.

"Jesus always speaks with love. He has compassion on the sorrow of the widow of Naim, on the misery of the lepers; he has mercy, above all, with the sinner. Jesus is expertly tactful, in saying an encouraging word, in corresponding to friendship with friendship in return. What conversations those in the house of Bethany, with Lazarus, Martha, and Mary!

"But Jesus also knows how to be demanding, knows how to get people to face their duties squarely, even at the risk of being spurned. See how the heart of Christ is shown in his concern for the rich young man who approaches him on one occasion: Jesus

Christ and the Samaritan Woman, *Venice, San Marco.*

VENITE · VIDETE · HOEM · OЪ · M DI
O MIA · ONE · FECI

looks upon him with love, while he asks of him detachment from his riches. *Qui contristatus in verbo abiit moerens,* the adolescent went away sad, because the word of God—when it is not accepted—becomes as bitter as bile.

"Therefore, talk is not enough; we have to act, we have to put into practice the teaching we receive. Otherwise, dialogue—even dialogue with God—is not fruitful; because 'not everyone who says to me: Lord, Lord, will enter the kingdom of heaven, but those who do the will of my Father, they will enter.'

"Jesus is not moved by considerations of false prudence, nor by a deceitful politeness that would smooth over the hard edges of the truth. He talks, for instance, with some Pharisees who were after him *ut caperent eum in sermone,* to attack him using whatever words came out of his mouth. But he does not vacillate in speaking the truth, calling by name that which has no other name: Brood of vipers—he exclaims—how can you speak good, when you are evil? Another time it is he who initiates the dialogue, even if he is not being interrogated. Jesus speaks because he sees in his surroundings the need to give doctrine, to correct a twisted mentality: *Simon, habeo tibi aliquid dicere*; 'Simon, I have something to say to you.' Jesus does not understand dialogue as a concession that falsifies the truth.

"He is inclined to speak with everyone, even those who do not wish to know the truth, like Pilate: *Tu dicis quia rex sum ego.* ('You say that I am a king. For this I was born and for this I have come into the world: to give witness to the truth. Every one who is of the truth hears my voice.'). But—when the moment calls for it—he speaks without euphemisms, even harshly. At times tough actions accompany tough words: *And making a whip of cords, he drove them all . . . out of the temple.* Do not think that our Lord was irascible. He is *mitis et humilis corde,* meek and humble of heart; but he knows that the heart of man is sometimes as hard as bronze, and that only fire can melt it: the fire of love, the fire of the truth, the fire of the mission received from the Father. And so, the least symptom of good will, of desire to know that which is authentic, is reason enough for him to bend over backwards to enlighten, to bless, to praise."[13]

[13] "Letter of October 24, 1965," in *Studi Cattolici* 293/294 (1985).

THE BEATITUDES

"Seeing the crowds, he went up on the mountain, and when he sat down his disciples came to him. And he opened his mouth and taught them, saying: 'Blessed are the poor in spirit . . .' (Mt 5:1ff).

**The Sermon on
the Mount,**
*Beato Angelico
(1387–1455),
Florence,
Museum of
San Marco.*

The preaching of Saint Josemaría Escrivá was based on the word of Jesus Christ, and the Beatitudes form a principal part of that. He sought to help souls make the Word of God operative in their lives, to translate it into challenging but practical goals. The Beatitudes become, in his view, immediately feasible. The following texts are chosen from various works of his.

Blessed are the poor in spirit, for theirs is the kingdom of heaven.

"If you want to achieve this spirit, I would advise you to be sparing with yourself while being very generous towards others. Avoid unnecessary expenditure on luxuries and comforts, whether out of caprice, or vanity, etc. Don't create needs for yourself. In other words, learn from Saint Paul 'to live in poverty and to live in abundance, to be filled and to be hungry, to live in plenty and to live in want: I can do all things in him who comforts me. ' Like the Apostle, we too will come out winners in this spiritual combat if we keep our hearts unattached and free from ties."[14]

Blessed are those who mourn, for they shall be comforted.

"You enjoy an interior happiness and peace that you should not exchange for anything in the world. God is here. There is no better way than telling him our woes for them to cease being such."[15]

Blessed are the meek, they shall inherit the earth.

"It made me think when I heard that hard but true saying from a man of God, when he observed the haughtiness of a miserable creature: 'He wears the same skin as the devil—pride.'

"And there came to my mind, in contrast, a sincere desire to wrap myself in the virtue taught by Jesus Christ when he said, *Quia mitis sum et humilis corde*—I am meek and humble of heart. It was the virtue which attracted the gaze of the Most Holy Trinity to his Mother and our Mother: the humility of knowing and being aware of our nothingness."[16]

Blessed are those who hunger and thirst for righteousness, for they shall be satisfied.

"First of all, we must be just towards God. Let this fact be firmly impressed in our hearts, so that it shows in our behavior, for it is the touchstone of the true 'hunger and thirst for justice' which distinguishes this virtue from the shouting of the envious and resentful and from the outcries of the selfish and greedy . . . For the worst and most ungrateful injustice is to deny our Creator and Redeemer the recognition of the abundant and wonderful gifts he has given us. If you are really striving to be just, you will often reflect on your utter dependence upon God, and be filled with gratitude and the desire to repay the favors of a Father who loves us to the point of madness: 'For what have you got that you have not received?'"[17]

Blessed are the merciful, they shall obtain mercy.

"The life of Jesus Christ is a summary and compendium of the story of God's mercy: 'Blessed are the merciful, for they shall obtain mercy.' And on another occasion our Lord said: 'Be merciful, therefore, even as your Father in heaven is merciful.' Many other scenes of the Gospel have also made a deep impact on us, such as his forgiveness of the adulterous woman, the parable of the prodigal son, that of the lost sheep, that of the pardoned debtor, the resurrection of the son of the widow at Naim. . . . What security should be ours in considering the mercy of the Lord!"[18]

Blessed are the pure in heart, they shall see God.

"By divine vocation, some are called to live this purity in marriage. Others, foregoing all human love, are called to correspond solely and passionately to

God's love. Far from being slaves to sensuality, both the married and the unmarried are to be masters of their body and heart in order to give themselves unstintingly to others.

". . . Holy purity is not the only nor the principal Christian virtue. It is, however, essential if we are to persevere in the daily effort of our sanctification. If it is not lived, there can be no dedication to the apostolate. Purity is a consequence of the love that prompts us to commit to Christ our soul and body, our faculties and senses. It is not something negative; it is a joyful affirmation."[19]

Blessed are the peacemakers, for they shall be called sons of God.

"The task for a Christian is to drown evil in an abundance of good. It is not a question of negative campaigns, or of being *anti* anything. On the contrary, we should live positively, full of optimism, youthfulness, joy and peace. We should be understanding with all, with the followers of Christ and those who abandon him, or don't know him at all.

"But being understanding does not mean holding back, or remaining indifferent, but being active."[20]

Blessed are those who are persecuted for righteousness' sake, for theirs is the kingdom of heaven.

"Contempt and persecution are blessed signs of divine predilection, but there is no proof and sign of predilection more beautiful than this: to pass unnoticed."[21]

Blessed are you when men revile you and persecute you and utter all kinds of evil against you falsely on my account. Rejoice and be glad, for your reward is great in heaven.

"When we think we have been accused of something unjustly, we should examine our behavior, in God's presence, *cum gaudio et pace*—calmly and cheerfully; and we should change our ways if charity bids us, even if our actions were harmless.

"We have to struggle to be saints, more and more each day. Then let people say what they like so long as we can apply the words of the beatitude to their utterances: *Beati estis cum . . . dixerint omne malum adversus vos mentientes propter me*—Blessed are you when they slander you for my sake."[22]

---

14 *Friends of God,* 123.
15 *The Forge,* no. 54
16 *Furrow,* no. 726.
17 *Friends of God,* 167.
18 *Christ Is Passing By,* 7.

19 *Christ Is Passing By,* 5.
20 *Furrow,* no. 864.
21 *The Way,* no. 959.
22 *The Forge,* no. 795.

Inside the Gospel

THE COMPASSION OF JESUS

"Soon afterwards he went to a city called Naim, and his disciples and a great crowd went with him. As he drew near to the gate of the city, behold, a man who had died was being carried out, the only son of his mother, and she was a widow; and a large crowd from the city was with her.

And when the Lord saw her, he had compassion on her and said to her, 'Do not weep.' And he came and touched the bier, and the bearers stood still. And he said, 'Young man, I say to you, arise.' And the dead man sat up, and began to speak. And he gave him to his mother.

Fear seized them all; and they glorified God,

The Resurrection of Lazarus, *Santi di Tito (1536–1603), Florence, Santa Maria Novella.*

saying, '*A great prophet has arisen among us!' and
'God has visited his people!'*" (*Lk* 7:11–16).

"Do you remember the scene Saint Luke depicts
when Jesus is approaching Naim? Jesus crosses paths
again with a crowd of people. He could have passed
by or waited until they called him. But he didn't. He
took the initiative, because he was moved by a
widow's sorrow. She had just lost all she had, her son.

"The evangelist explains that Jesus was moved.
Perhaps he even showed signs of it, as when Lazarus
died. Jesus Christ was not, and is not, insensitive to
the suffering that stems from love. He is pained at
seeing children separated from their parents. He
overcomes death so as to give life, to reunite those
who love one another. But at the same time, he requires that we first admit the pre-eminence of divine
love, which alone can inspire genuine Christian living.

"Christ knows he is surrounded by a crowd which
will be awed by the miracle and will tell the story all
over the countryside. But he does not act artificially,
merely for effect. Quite simply he is touched by that
woman's suffering and cannot keep from consoling
her. So he goes up to her and says, 'Do not weep.' It is
like saying: 'I don't want to see you crying; I have come
on earth to bring joy and peace.' And then comes the
miracle, the sign of the power of Christ who is God.
But first came his compassion, an evident sign of the
tenderness of the heart of Christ the man.

"If we don't learn from Jesus, we will never love.
If, like some people, we were to think that to keep a
clean heart, a heart worthy of God, means 'not mixing
it up, not contaminating it' with human affection,
we would become insensitive to other people's pain
and sorrow. We would be capable only of an 'official
charity,' something dry and soulless. But ours would
not be the true charity of Jesus Christ, which in-
volves affection and human warmth. In saying this,
I am not supporting the mistaken theories—sad
excuses—which misdirect hearts away from God
and lead them into occasions of sin and perdition.

". . . If we want to help others, we must love
them—I insist—with a love clothed in understanding,
dedication, affection and voluntary humility. Then
we will understand why our Lord summed up the
whole law in that double commandment, which is
really just one: love of God, and love of one's neighbor, with all our heart."[23]

[23] *Christ Is Passing By,* 166–167

PARABLE OF THE SOWER

"And when a great crowd came together and people from town after town came to him, he said in a parable: 'A sower went out to sow his seed; and as he sowed, some fell along the path, and was trodden under foot, and the birds of the air devoured it. . . . Now the parable is this: The seed is the word of God. The ones along the path are those who have heard; then the devil comes and takes away the

The Sower,
*Ivan Grohar
(1867–1911),
Ljubljana, Gallery
of Modern Art.*

word from their hearts, that they may not believe and be saved.'" (*Lk* 8:4–5, 11–12).

"Some hearts close themselves to the light of faith. Ideals of peace, reconciliation and brotherhood are widely accepted, but all too often the facts belie them. Some people are futilely bent on smothering God's voice. To drown it out they use brute force or a method which is more subtle but perhaps more cruel because it drugs the spirit, indifference."[24]

"And some fell on the rock; and as it grew up, it withered away, . . . The ones on the rock are those who, when they hear the word, receive it with joy; but these have no root, they believe for a while and in time of temptation fall away" (*Lk* 8:6 and 13).

"You may perhaps have noticed . . . many people

who call themselves Christians because they have been baptized and have received other sacraments, but then prove to be disloyal and deceitful, insincere and proud, and . . . they fail to achieve anything. They are like shooting stars, lighting up the sky for an instant and then falling away to nothing.

"If we accept the responsibility of being children of God, we will realize that God wants us to be very human. Our heads should indeed be touching heaven, but our feet should be firmly on the ground. The price of living as Christians is not that of ceasing to be human or of abandoning the effort to acquire those virtues which some have even without knowing Christ. The price paid for each Christian is the redeeming Blood of Our Lord and he, I insist, wants us to be both very human and very divine, struggling each day to imitate him who is *perfectus Deus, perfectus homo.*"[25]

"And some fell among thorns; and the thorns grew with it and choked it. . . . And as for what fell among the thorns, they are those who hear, but as they go on their way they are choked by the cares and riches and pleasures of life, and their fruit does not mature" (Lk 8:7 and 14).

"Do not be ashamed to discover in your heart the *fomes peccati*—the inclination to evil, which will be with you as long as you live, for nobody is free from this burden.

"Do not be ashamed, for the all-powerful and merciful Lord has given us all the means we need for overcoming this inclination: the sacraments, a life of piety and sanctified work..

"Persevere in using these means, ever ready to begin again and again without getting discouraged."[26]

"And some fell into good soil and grew, and yielded a hundred-fold.... They are those who, hearing the word, hold it fast in an honest and good heart, and bring forth fruit with patience." (Lk 8:8 and 15).

"If we look around, if we take a look at the world, which we love because it is God's handiwork, we will find that the parable holds true. The word of Jesus Christ is fruitful, it stirs many souls to dedication and fidelity. The life and conduct of those who serve God have changed history. Even many of those who do not know our Lord are motivated, perhaps unconsciously, by ideals which come from Christianity."[27]

---

[24] *Christ Is Passing By,* 150.
[25] *Friends of God,* 75.
[26] *The Forge,* 119.
[27] *Christ Is Passing By,* 150.

THE MUTE DEVIL

*"And when they came to the disciples, they saw
a great crowd about them, and the scribes arguing
with them. . . . And he asked them, 'what are you discussing with them?' And one of the crowd answered
him. 'Teacher, I brought my son to you for he has a
dumb spirit; and wherever it seizes him, it dashes
him down; and he foams and grinds his teeth and
becomes rigid; and I asked your disciples to cast it
out, and they were not able.' And he answered
them, 'O faithless generation, how long am I to be
with you? How long am I to bear with you? Bring
him to me.' And they brought the boy to him; and
when the spirit saw him, immediately it convulsed
the boy, and he fell on the ground and rolled about,
foaming at the mouth. And Jesus asked his father,
'How long has he had this?' And he said, 'From
childhood. And it has often cast him into the fire
and into the water, to destroy him; but if you can do
anything, have pity on us and help us.' And Jesus
said to him, 'If you can! All things are possible to
him who believes.' Immediately the father of the
child cried out and said, 'I believe; help my unbelief!'
And when Jesus saw that a crowd came running
together, he rebuked the unclean spirit, saying to it,
'You dumb and deaf spirit, I command you, come
out of him, and never enter him again.' And after
crying out and convulsing him terribly, it came out,
and the boy was like a corpse; so that most of them
said, 'He is dead.' But Jesus took him by the hand
and lifted him up, and he arose. And when he had
entered the house, his disciples asked him privately,
'Why could we not cast it out?' And he said to them,
'This kind cannot be driven out by anything but
prayer and fasting.'"* (Mk 9:14–29).

"Just because we discover how fragile we are is
no reason to run away from God. What we must do
is to attack our defects, precisely because we know
that God trusts us.

"How shall we be able to overcome our mean-
ness? Let me make the point again because it is so
important: by being humble and by being sincere in
spiritual direction and in the sacrament of Penance.
Go to those who direct your souls with your hearts
open wide. Do not close your hearts, for if the dumb
devil gets in, it is very difficult to get rid of him.

*The
Transfiguration*
(detail from the
Cure of the
Mute Child),
Raffaello Sanzio
(1483–1520),
Vatican Museum.

"Forgive me for insisting on these points, but I believe it is absolutely necessary for you to have deeply impressed on your minds the fact that humility, together with its immediate consequence, sincerity, are the thread which links the other means together. These two virtues act as a foundation on which a solid victory can be built. If the dumb devil gets inside a soul, he ruins everything. On the other hand, if he is cast out immediately, everything turns out well; we are happy and life goes forward properly. Let us always be *brutally sincere,* but in a good-mannered way.

"I want one thing to be clear: I am not as worried about the heart or the flesh as I am about pride. Be humble. If you ever think that you are completely and utterly right, you are not right at all. Go to spiritual direction with your soul wide open. Don't close it because, I repeat, the dumb devil will get in, and it is difficult to get him out again.

"Remember the poor boy who was possessed by a devil, and the disciples were unable to set him free. Only our Lord could free him, by prayer and fasting. Here the Master worked three miracles. The first enabled the boy to hear because, when the dumb devil gets control, the soul refuses to listen. The second made him speak, and the third expelled the devil.

"Tell first what you would not like to be known. Down with the dumb devil! By turning some small matter over and over in your mind, you will make it snowball into something big, with you trapped inside. What's the point of doing that? Open up your soul! I promise that you will be happy, that is, faithful to your Christian way, if you are sincere. Clarity and simplicity: they are absolutely necessary dispositions. We have to open up our souls completely, so that the God's sunshine and the charity of Love can enter in.

"It is not necessarily bad will that prevents people from being utterly sincere. Sometimes they may simply have an erroneous conscience. Some people have so formed, or rather deformed, their consciences that they think their inability to speak, their lack of simplicity, is something good. They think it is good to remain silent. This can even happen to people who have received an excellent training and know the things of God. This may indeed be what is convincing them that they should not speak out. But they are wrong. Sincerity is a must, always. There are no valid excuses, no matter how good they seem."[28]

[28] *Friends of God,* 187–189.

LIKE CHILDREN

"And they came to Capernaum; and when he was in the house he asked them, 'What were you discussing on the way?' But they were silent; for on the way they had discussed with one another who was the greatest. And he sat down and called the twelve; and he said to them, 'If any one would be first, he must be last of all and servant of all.'

"And he took a child, and put him in the midst of them; and taking him in his arms, he said to them, 'Whoever receives one such child in my name receives me; and whoever receives me, receives not

Tobias and the Archangel Raphael, *School of Titian, Venice, Academy.*

me but him who sent me'" (Mk 9:33–37).

"Doesn't this way Jesus has of doing things move us to love him? He teaches them the doctrine and then, to enable them to understand it, he gives them a living example. He calls a little child, one of the children running around the house, and he lovingly embraces him. How eloquent Our Lord's silence is! With it he has already said everything. He loves those who become as little children. He then adds that the reward for this simplicity, for this humility of spirit, is the joy of being able to embrace him and his Father who is in heaven."[29]

"At that time the disciples came to Jesus, saying, 'Who is the greatest in the kingdom of heaven?' And calling to him a child, he put him in the midst of them, and said, 'Truly, I say to you, unless you turn and become like children, you will never enter the kingdom of heaven. Whoever humbles himself like this child, he is the greatest in the kingdom of heaven.'" (Mk 9:33–37).

"To become children we must renounce our pride and self-sufficiency, recognizing that we can do nothing by ourselves. We must realize that we need grace, and the help of God our Father to find our way and keep to it. To be little, you have to abandon yourself as children do, believe as children believe, beg as children beg.

"And we learn all this through contact with Mary. . . . Because Mary is our mother, devotion to her teaches us to be authentic children: to love truly, without limit; to be simple, without the complications which come from selfishly thinking only about ourselves; to be happy, knowing that nothing can destroy our hope. The beginning of the way, at the end of which you will find yourself completely carried away by love for Jesus, is a trusting love for Mary."[30]

"What a wonderful thing it is to be a child! When a man asks a favor, his request must be backed by a list of his qualifications.

"When it is a child who asks—since children haven't any qualifications—it's enough for him to say: I'm a son of So-and-so.

"Ah, Lord,—say it to him with all your heart! —I am a son of God!"[31]

[29] *Friends of God,* 102.   [31] *The Way,* 892.
[30] *Christ is Passing By,* 143.

THE GOOD SHEPHERD

"Truly, truly, I say to you, he who does not enter the sheepfold by the door but climbs in by another way, that man is a thief and a robber; but he who enters by the door is the shepherd of the sheep. To him the gatekeeper opens; the sheep hear his voice, and he calls his own sheep by name and leads them out. When he has brought out all his own, he goes before them, and the sheep follow him, for they know his voice. A stranger they will not follow, but they will flee from him, for they do not know the voice of strangers . . .

Truly, truly, I say to you, I am the door of the sheep . . .

If any one enters by me, he will be saved, and will go in and out and find pasture . . .

The Good Shepherd, *Ravenna, Mausoleum of Gallia Placidia.*

I am the good shepherd. The good shepherd lays down his life for the sheep" (*Jn* 10:1–11).

"I remember, many years ago now, I was going along a road in Castile with some friends, when we noticed something in a field far away which made a deep impression on me at the time and has since often helped me in my prayer. A group of men were hammering some wooden stakes into the ground, which they then used to support netting to form a sheep pen. Then shepherds came along with their sheep and their lambs. They called them by their names and one by one lambs and sheep went into the pen, where they would be all together, safe and sound.

"Today, Lord, my thoughts go back particularly to those shepherds and their sheepfold, because all of us who are gathered here to converse with you—and many others the world over—we all know that we have been brought into your sheepfold. You yourself have told us so: 'I am the Good Shepherd. I know my sheep and my sheep know me.' You know us well. You know that we wish to hear, to listen ever attentively to your gentle whistling as our Good Shepherd, and to heed it, because 'eternal life is knowing you, who are the only true God, and Jesus Christ whom you have sent.'

"The image of Christ with his sheep at his right and left means so much to me that I had it depicted in the oratory where I normally celebrate Holy Mass. Elsewhere, as a reminder of God's presence, I have had engraved Jesus' words, *cognosco oves meas et cognoscunt me meae* ('I know my sheep, and my sheep know me'), to help us consider constantly that he is at our side, reproaching us, instructing us and teaching us as a shepherd does with his flock."[32]

"Christ has given his Church sureness in doctrine and a flow of grace in the sacraments. He has arranged things so that there will always be people to guide and lead us, to remind us constantly of our way. There is an infinite treasure of knowledge available to us: the word of God kept safe by the Church, the grace of Christ administered in the sacraments and also the witness and example of those who live by our side and have known how to build with their good lives a road of faithfulness to God. . . .

"The holiness of Christ's Spouse has always been shown—as it can be seen today—by the abundance of good shepherds. But our Christian faith, which teaches us to be simple, does not bid us be simple-minded. There are hirelings who keep silent, and there are hirelings who speak with words which are not those of Christ. That is why, if the Lord allows us to be left in the dark even in little things, if we feel that our faith is not firm, we should go to the good shepherd. He enters by the door as of right. He gives his life for others and wants to be in word and behavior a soul in love. He may be a sinner too, but he trusts always in Christ's forgiveness and mercy."[33]

[32] *Friends of God*, 1.   [33] *Christ is Passing By*, 34.

THE PRAYER OF JESUS

*"And in the morning, a great while before day,
he rose and went out to a lonely place, and there he
prayed. And Simon and those who were with him
followed him, and they found him and said to him,
'Everyone is searching for you.'"* (Mk 1:35–37).

*"In these days he went out into the hills to
pray; and all night he continued in prayer to God.
And when it was day, he called his disciples, and
chose from them twelve, whom he named apostles"*
(*Lk* 6:12–13).

*Jesus in the
Garden of
Olives, Francisco
de Goya
(1746–1828),
Paris, Louvre
Museum.*

"It is very important to note carefully what the
Messiah did, because he came to show us the path
that leads to the Father. With our Lord we will discover how to give a supernatural dimension to all
our actions, even those that seem least important.
We will learn to live every moment of our lives with

a lively awareness of eternity, and we will understand more deeply man's need for periods of intimate conversation with his God, so as to get to know him, to call on him, to praise him, to break out into acts of thanksgiving, to listen to him or, quite simply, to be with him.

"Many years ago, as I reflected upon our Lord's way of doing things, I came to the conclusion that the apostolate, of whatever kind it be, must be an overflow of the interior life. This is why the passage, which relates how Christ decided to choose the first twelve, seems to me to be so natural and at the same time so supernatural. Saint Luke tells us that before choosing them 'he spent the whole night in prayer.' Think also of the events at Bethany. Before he raises Lazarus from the dead, after having wept over his friend, he lifts his eyes to heaven and says, 'Father, I thank you for hearing my prayer.' This is his message for us: if we wish to help others, if we really wish to encourage them to discover the true meaning of their life on earth, we must base everything on prayer.

"There are so many Gospel scenes where Jesus talks to his Father that we cannot stop to consider them all. But I do feel we must pause to consider the intense hours preceding his Passion and Death, when Christ prepares to carry out the Sacrifice that will bring us back once more to God's Love. In the intimacy of the Upper Room the Heart of Jesus overflows with love; he turns to the Father in prayer, announces the coming of the Holy Spirit, and encourages his disciples to maintain the fervor of their charity and their faith.

"Our Redeemer's mood of fervent recollection continues in the Garden of Gethsemani, as he perceives that his Passion is about to begin, with all its humiliation and suffering close at hand, the harsh cross on which criminals are hanged and which he has longed for so ardently. 'Father, if it pleases thee, take away this chalice from before me.' And immediately he adds, 'Yet not my will but thine be done.' Later, nailed to the Cross, alone, with his arms opened wide in a gesture of an eternal priest, he continues his dialogue with his Father, 'Into thy hands I commend my spirit.'"[34]

[34] *Friends of God*, 239–240

THE PRODIGAL SON

"But while he was yet at a distance, his father saw him and had compassion, and ran and embraced him and kissed him. And the son said to him, 'Father, I have sinned against heaven and before you; I am no longer worthy to be called your son.'

But the father said to his servants, 'Bring quickly the best robe, and put it on him; and put a ring on his hand, and shoes on his feet; and bring the fatted calf and kill it, and let us eat and make merry; for this my son was dead and is alive again; he was lost, and is found.' And they began to make merry" (Lk 15:20–24).

The Return of the Prodigal Son, *Rembrandt (1606–1669), St. Petersburg, Hermitage Museum.*

"'But while he was still a long way off, his father saw him and took pity on him; running up, he threw his arms around his neck and kissed him.' That's what the sacred text says: he covered him with kisses. Can you put it more humanly than that? Can you describe more graphically the paternal love of God for men?

"When God runs toward us, we cannot keep silent, but with Saint Paul we exclaim: *Abba, Pater*: 'Father, my Father!,' for, though he is the creator of the universe, he doesn't mind our not using high-sounding titles, nor worry about our not acknowledging his greatness. He wants us to call him Father; he wants us to savor that word, our souls filling with joy.

"Human life is in some way a constant returning to our Father's house. We return through contrition, through the conversion of heart which means a desire to change, a firm decision to improve our life and which, therefore, is expressed in sacrifice and self-giving. We return to our Father's house by means of that sacrament of pardon in which, by confessing our sins, we put on Jesus Christ again and become his brothers, members of God's family.

"God is waiting for us, like the father in the parable, with open arms, even though we don't deserve it. It doesn't matter how great our debt is. Just like the prodigal son, all we have to do is open our heart, to be homesick for our Father's house, to wonder at and rejoice in the gift which God makes us of being able to call ourselves his children, of really being his children, even though our response to him has been so poor."[35]

"For a Christian, joy is a treasure. Only by offending God do we lose it, because sin is the fruit of selfishness, and selfishness is the root of sadness. Even then, a bit of joy survives under the debris of our soul: the knowledge that neither God nor his Mother can ever forget us. If we repent, if an act of sorrow springs from our heart, if we purify ourselves in the holy sacrament of penance, God comes out to meet and forgive us. Then there can be no sadness whatsoever. Then there is every right 'to rejoice, because your brother was dead and has come back to life, was lost and has been found.' These words are taken from the marvelous ending of the parable of the prodigal son, which we shall never tire of meditating."[36]

[35] *Christ Is Passing By,* 64.   [36] *Christ Is Passing By,* 178.

BARTIMAEUS

"And they came to Jericho; and as he was leaving Jericho with his disciples and a great multitude, Bartimaeus, a blind beggar, the son of Timaeus, was sitting by the roadside. And when he heard that it was Jesus of Nazareth, he began to cry out and say, 'Jesus, Son of David, have mercy on me!'" (Mk 10:46–47).

**The Cure of
the Blind Man,**
*El Greco
(1541–1614).
Parma, National
Gallery.*

"I recommend that you meditate slowly on the events preceding the miracle, to help you keep this fundamental idea clearly engraved upon your minds: what a world of difference there is between the merciful Heart of Jesus and our own poor hearts! This thought will help you at all times, and especially in the hour of trial and temptation, and also when the time comes to be generous in the little duties you have, or in moments when heroism is called for.

"'Many of them rebuked him, telling him to be silent' (*Mk* 10:48). As people have done to you, when you sensed that Jesus was passing your way. Your heart beat faster and you too began to cry out, prompted by an intimate longing. Then your friends, the need to do the fashionable thing, the easy life, your surroundings, all conspired to tell you: 'Keep quiet, don't cry out. Who are you to be calling Jesus? Don't bother him.'

"But poor Bartimaeus would not listen to them. He cried out all the more: 'Son of David, have pity on me.' Our Lord, who had heard him right from the beginning, let him persevere in his prayer. He does the same with you. Jesus hears our cries from the very first, but he waits. He wants us to be convinced that we need him. He wants us to beseech him, to persist, like the blind man waiting by the road from Jericho.

"'And Jesus stopped, and told them to call him.' Some of the better people in the crowd turned to the blind man and said, 'Take heart. Rise up, he is calling you' (*Mk* 10:49). Here you have the Christian vocation! But God does not call only once. Bear in mind that our Lord is seeking us at every moment: get up, he tells us, put aside your indolence, your easy life, your petty selfishness, your silly little problems. Get up from the ground, where you are lying prostrate and out of shape. Acquire height, weight and volume, and a supernatural outlook.

"'Whereupon the man threw away his cloak and leapt to his feet, and so came to him.' (*Mk* 10:50). He threw aside his cloak! I don't know if you have ever lived through a war, but many years ago I had occasion to visit a battlefield shortly after an engagement. There, strewn all over the ground, were overcoats, water bottles, haversacks stuffed with family souvenirs, letters, photographs of loved ones . . . which belonged, moreover, not to the vanquished, but to the victors! All these items had become superfluous in the bid to race forward and leap over the enemy defenses. Just as happened to Bartimaeus, as he raced towards Christ.

"Never forget that Christ cannot be reached without sacrifice. We have to get rid of everything that gets in the way: overcoat, haversack, water bottle. You have to do the same in this battle for the glory of God, in this struggle of love and peace by which we are trying to spread Christ's kingdom. In order to serve the Church, the Pope and all souls, you must be ready to give up everything super-fluous, to be left without a cloak to shelter you from the bitter cold of night, without your much loved family souvenirs, without water to refresh you. This is the lesson taught us by faith and love. This is the way that we must love Christ.

"And now begins a dialogue with God, a marvelous dialogue that moves us and sets our hearts on fire, for you and I are now Bartimaeus. Christ, who is God, begins to speak and asks, *Quid tibi vis faciam?* 'What do you want me to do for you?' The blind man answers, 'Lord, that I may see.' (*Mk* 10:51). How utterly logical! How about yourself, can you really see? Haven't you too experienced at times what happened to the blind man of Jericho? I can never forget how, when meditating on this passage many years back, and realizing that Jesus was expecting something of me, though I myself did not know what it was, I made up my own aspirations: 'Lord, what is it you want? What are you asking of me'? I had a feeling that he wanted me to take on something new and the cry *Rabboni, ut videam,* 'Master, that I may see,' moved me to beseech Christ again and again, 'Lord, whatever it is that you wish, let it be done.'

"But let us go back to the scene outside Jericho. It is now to you that Christ is speaking. He asks you, 'What is it you want of me?' 'That I may see, Lord, that I may see.' Then Jesus answers, 'Go. Your faith has brought you recovery. And all at once he recovered his sight and followed Jesus on his way.' (*Mk* 10:52) Following Jesus on his way. You have understood what our Lord was asking from you and you have decided to accompany him on his way. You are trying to walk in his footsteps, to clothe yourself in Christ's clothing, to be Christ himself: well, your faith, your faith in the light our Lord is giving you, must be both operative and full of sacrifice. Don't fool yourself. Don't think you are going to find new ways. The faith he demands of us is as I have said. We must keep in step with him, working generously and at the same time uprooting and getting rid of everything that gets in the way."[37]

[37] *Friends of God,* 195–198.

THE NEW COMMANDMENT

"Now before the feast of the Passover, when Jesus knew that his hour had come to depart out of this world to the Father, having loved his own who were in the world, he loved them to the end" (*Jn* 13:1).

"The reader of this verse from Saint John's Gospel is brought to understand that a great event is about to take place. The introduction, full of tender affection, is similar to that which we find in Saint Luke: 'I have earnestly desired,' says our Lord, 'to eat this Passover with you before I suffer' (*Lk* 22:15)."[38]

"Now it is the Last Supper. Christ has prepared everything to bid farewell to his disciples, while they, for the umpteenth time, have become embroiled in

The Washing of the Feet,
Flemish work, Trent, Cathedral.

an argument about which one of the chosen group is to be considered the greatest. Jesus then 'rising from supper, laid his garments aside, took a towel and put it about him. Then he poured water into a basin and began to wash the feet of his disciples, wiping them with the towel that girded him' (*Jn* 13:4–5).

"Once again he preaches by example, by his deeds. In the presence of the disciples, who are arguing out of pride and vanity, Jesus bows down and gladly carries out the task of a servant. Afterwards, when he returns to the table, he explains to them: 'Do you understand what it is I have done to you? You call me Master and Lord, and you are right; it is what I am. Why then, if I have washed your feet, I who am the Master and the Lord, you in your turn ought to wash each other's feet.' (*Jn* 13:12–14). This tactfulness of our Lord moves me deeply. He does not say: 'If I do this, how much more ought you to.' He puts himself at their level, and he lovingly chides those men for their lack of generosity.

"As he did with the first twelve, so also, with us, our Lord can and does whisper in our ear, time and again, *exemplum dedi vobis* (*Jn* 13:15), I have given you an example of humility. I have become a slave, so that you too may learn to serve all men with a meek and humble heart."[39]

"The time of his Passion is drawing close and he is surrounded by those he loves. The fire in the Heart of Christ bursts into flame in a way no words can express and he confides in them, 'I give you a new commandment that you love one another; just as I have loved you, you also must love one another. By this shall all men know that you are my disciples, if you have love for one another' (*Jn* 13: 34–35). . . .

"Lord, why do you call it a *new* commandment? As we have just heard, it was already laid down in the Old Testament that we should love our neighbor. You will remember also that, when Jesus had scarcely begun his public life, he broadened the scope of this law with divine generosity: 'You have heard that it was said, You shall love your neighbor and hate your enemy. But I tell you, Love your enemies, do good to those who hate you, pray for those who persecute and slander you' (*Mt* 5:43–44).

"But, Lord, please allow us to insist. Why do you still call this precept new? That night, just a few hours before offering yourself in sacrifice on the Cross, during your intimate conversation with the men who—in spite of being weak and wretched, like ourselves—accompanied you to Jerusalem, you revealed to us the standard for our charity, one we could never have suspected: 'as I have loved you.' How well the apostles must have understood you, having witnessed for themselves your unbounded love. The Master's message and example are clear and precise. He confirmed his teaching with deeds.

". . . Our Lord Jesus Christ became incarnate and took on our nature to reveal himself to mankind as the model of all virtues, 'Learn from me,' he says to us, 'for I am meek and humble of heart' (*Mt* 11:29).

"Later, when he explains to the apostles the mark by which they will be known as Christians, he does not say, 'Because you are humble.' He is purity most sublime, the immaculate Lamb. Nothing could stain his perfect, unspotted holiness. Yet he does not say, 'You will be known as my disciples because you are chaste and pure.'

"He passed through this world completely detached from earthly goods. Though he is the Creator and Lord of the whole universe, he did not even have a place to lay his head. Nevertheless he does not say, 'They will know that you are mine because you are not attached to wealth.' Before setting out to preach the Gospel he spent forty days and forty nights in the desert keeping a strict fast. But, once again, he does not tell his disciples, 'Men will recognize you as God's servants because you are not gluttons or drunkards.'

"No, the distinguishing mark of the apostles and of true Christians in every age is, as we have heard: 'By this,' precisely by this, 'shall all men know that you are my disciples, if you have love for one another.'"[40]

[38] *Christ Is Passing By*, 83.   [40] *Friends of God*, 222–224.
[39] *Friends of God*, 103.

THE EUCHARIST

*"And he took bread, and when he had given
thanks he broke it and gave it to them, saying, 'This
is my body which is given for you. Do this in memory of me.' And likewise the cup after supper, saying,
'This cup which is poured out for you is the new
covenant in my blood.'"* (Lk 22:19–20).

"Think of the human experience of two people
who love each other, and yet are forced to part. They
would like to stay together forever, but duty—in one
form or another—forces them to separate. They are
unable to fulfill their desire of remaining close to
each other, so man's love—which, great as it may be,
is limited—seeks a symbolic gesture. People who
make their farewells exchange gifts or perhaps a
photograph with a dedication so ardent that it seems
almost enough to burn that piece of paper. They can
do no more, because a creature's power is not so
great as its desire.

"What we cannot do, our Lord is able to do.
Jesus Christ, perfect God and perfect man, leaves us,
not a symbol, but a reality. He himself stays with us.
He will go to the Father, but he will also remain
among men. He will leave us, not simply a gift that
will make us remember him, not an image that becomes blurred with time, like a photograph that soon
fades and yellows, and has no meaning except for
those who were contemporaries. Under the appear-
ances of bread and wine, he is really present, with
his body and blood, with his soul and divinity."[41]

"The miracle of the holy Eucharist is being continually renewed and it has all Jesus' personal traits.
Perfect God and perfect man, Lord of heaven and
earth, he offers himself to us as nourishment in the
most natural and ordinary way. Love has been awaiting us for almost two thousand years. That's a long
time and yet it's not, for when you are in love time
flies.

"I remember a lovely poem, one of the songs
collected by King Alfonso the Wise. It's a legend
about a simple monk who begged our Lady to let
him see heaven, even if only for a moment. Our
Lady granted him his wish and the good monk

found himself in paradise. When he returned, he could not recognize the monastery—his prayer, which he had thought very short, lasted three centuries. Three centuries are nothing to a person in love. That's how I explain Christ waiting in the Eucharist. It is God waiting for us, God who loves man, who searches us out, who loves us just as we are—limited, selfish, inconstant, but capable of discovering his infinite affection and of giving ourselves fully to him. . . .

"This is a miracle of love. 'This is truly the bread for God's children.' Jesus, the first son of the eternal Father, offers us himself as food. And the same Jesus is waiting to receive us in heaven as 'his guests, his co-heirs and his fellows,' for 'those who are nourished by Christ will die the earthly death of time, but they will live eternally because Christ is life everlasting.'

". . . Jesus hides in the blessed Sacrament of the altar because he wants us to *dare* to approach him. He wants to nourish us so we become one single thing with him. When he said, 'Apart from me you can do nothing,' he was not condemning Christians to ineffectiveness or obliging them to seek him by a

difficult and arduous route. On the contrary. He has stayed here with us, he is totally available to us. . . .

"When we meet together around the altar to celebrate the holy sacrifice of the Mass, when we contemplate the sacred host in the monstrance or adore Him hidden in the tabernacle, our faith should be strengthened; we should reflect on this new life which we are receiving and be moved by God's affection and tenderness. . . .

"For me the tabernacle has always been a Bethany, a quiet and pleasant place where Christ resides. A place where we can tell him about our worries, our sufferings, our desires, our joys, with the same sort of simplicity and naturalness as Martha, Mary and Lazarus. That is why I rejoice when I stumble upon a church in town or in the country; it's another tabernacle, another opportunity for the soul to escape and join in intention our Lord in the Sacrament."[42]

The Last Supper, Leonardo da Vinci (1452–1519), Milan, Santa Maria delle Grazie.

[41] *Christ Is Passing By,* 83.
[42] *Christ Is Passing By,* 151–154.

THE PASSION

"From that time Jesus began to show his disciples that he must go to Jerusalem and suffer many things from the elders and chief priests and scribes, and be killed, and on the third day be raised" (Mt 16:21).

The Crowning with Thorns,
Alonso del Arco (1625–1700), Rome.

"Pilate speaks: It is your custom that I release one prisoner to you on the Pasch. Whom shall I set free, Barabbas—a thief jailed with others for a murder —or Jesus? —Put this man to death and release unto us Barabbas, cries the multitude, incited by their chief priests.

Pilate speaks again: What shall I do, then, with Jesus, who is called Christ? —*Crucifige eum!* Crucify Him!

Pilate, for the third time, says to them: Why, what evil has He done? I find no fault in Him that deserves death.

The clamor of the mob grows louder: Crucify Him, crucify Him!

And Pilate, wishing to please the populace, releases Barabbas to them and orders Jesus to be scourged.

Bound to the pillar. Covered with wounds.

The blows of the lash sound upon His torn flesh, upon His undefiled flesh, that suffers for your sinful flesh. —More blows. More fury. Still more . . . It is the last extreme of human cruelty.

Finally, exhausted, they unbind Jesus. —And the body of Christ yields to pain and falls limp, broken and half dead.

You and I are unable to speak. —Words are not needed. —Look at Him, look at Him . . . slowly. After this . . . can you ever fear penance?"[43]

"Our King's eagerness for suffering has been fully satisfied! —They lead Our Lord to the court-yard of the palace, and there they call together their whole band. The brutal soldiers strip His most pure body. They drape a dirty purple rag about Jesus. A reed, as a scepter, in His right hand . . .

The crown of thorns, driven in by blows, makes Him a mock king . . . *Ave Rex Judaeorum!* —Hail, King of the Jews. (And with their blows they wound His head. And they strike Him . . . and they spit on Him.

Crowned with thorns and clothed in rags of purple, Jesus is shown to the Jewish mob: *Ecce Homo!* —Behold the Man! And again the chief priests and the ministers raise the cry, saying: Crucify Him, crucify Him.

—You and I . . ., haven't we crowned Him anew with thorns, and struck Him and spit on Him?

Never more, Jesus, never more . . ."[44]

"Carrying His Cross, Jesus goes out toward Calvary, a place that in Hebrew is called Golgotha.

The prophesy of Isaiah has been fulfilled: *cum sceleratis reputatus est,* He was counted among the wicked: for two others, who were robbers, were led with Him to be put to death.

If anyone would follow me . . . Little friend: we are sad, living the Passion of Our Lord Jesus. —See how lovingly He embraces the Cross. —Learn from Him. —Jesus carries the Cross for you: you . . . carry it for Jesus.

But don't drag the Cross . . . Carry it squarely on your shoulder, because your Cross, if you carry it so, will not be just any Cross: it will be . . . the Holy Cross. Don't bear your Cross with resignation: resignation is not a generous word. Love the Cross. When you really love it, your Cross will be . . . a Cross without a Cross.

And surely you, like Him, will find Mary on the way."[45]

[43] *Holy Rosary,* second sorrowful mystery.
[44] *Holy Rosary,* third sorrowful mystery.
[45] *Holy Rosary,* fourth sorrowful mystery.

HIS DEATH ON THE CROSS

"So they took Jesus, and he went out, bearing his own cross, to the place called the place of a skull, which is called in Hebrew Golgotha. There they crucified him, and with him two others, one on either side, and Jesus between them. Pilate also wrote a title and put it on the cross; it read, 'Jesus of Nazareth, the King of the Jews'" (Jn 19:17–19).

The Crucifixion,
Giotto
(1266–1336),
Padua, Chapel
of the Scrovegni.

"Now they are crucifying Our Lord, and with him two thieves, one on his right and one on his left. Meanwhile, Jesus says:

Father, forgive them for they do not know what they are doing.

It is Love that has brought Jesus to Calvary. And once on the Cross, all his gestures and all his words are of love, a love both calm and strong. With a gesture befitting an Eternal Priest, without father or mother, without lineage, he opens his arms to the whole human race.

With the hammer blows with which Jesus is being nailed, there resound the prophetic words of Holy Scripture: *They have pierced my hands and* feet. *I can count all my bones, and they stare and gloat over me. My people, what have I done to thee, or in what have I saddened thee? Answer me!*

And we, our soul rent with sorrow, say to Jesus in all sincerity: I am yours and I give my whole self to You; gladly do I nail myself to your Cross, ready to be in the cross-roads of this world a soul dedicated to You, to your glory, to the work of Redemption, the co-redemption of the whole human race."

On the uppermost part of the Cross the reason for the sentence is written: *Jesus of Nazareth, King of the Jews.* And all who pass by insult him and jeer at him. *If he is the king of Israel, let him come down here and now from the cross.*

One of the thieves comes to his defense:
This man has done no evil . . .

Then, turning to Jesus, he makes a humble request, full of faith: *Lord, remember me when thou comest into thy kingdom.*

Truly, I say to thee: This day thou shalt be with me in Paradise.

At the foot of the Cross stands his Mother, Mary, with other holy women. Jesus looks at her; then he looks at the disciple whom he loves, and he says to his Mother: *Woman, behold thy son.*

Then he says to the disciple:
Behold thy mother.

The sun's light is extinguished and the earth is left in darkness. It is close on three o'clock, when Jesus cries out:

Eli, Eli, lamma sabacthani? That is: My God, my God, why hast thou forsaken me?

Then, knowing that all things are about to be accomplished, that the Scriptures may be fulfilled, he says: *I am thirsty.*

The soldiers soak a sponge in vinegar and, placing it on a reed of hyssop, they put it to his mouth. Jesus sips the vinegar, and exclaims:
It is accomplished.

The veil of the temple is rent, and the earth trembles, when the Lord cries out in a loud voice:
Father, into thy hands I commend my spirit.
And he expires.

Love sacrifice; it is a fountain of interior life. Love the Cross, which is an altar of sacrifice. Love pain, until you drink, as Christ did, the very dregs of the chalice."[46]

---

[46] *The Way of the Cross,* Eleventh and Twelfth Stations.

THE RESURRECTION

"On the evening of that day, the first day of the week, the doors being shut where the disciples were, for fear of the Jews, Jesus came and stood among them and said to them, 'Peace be with you.' When he had said this, he showed them his hands and his side. Then the disciples were glad when they saw the Lord. Jesus said to them again, 'Peace be with you. As the Father has sent me, even so I send you.' And when he had said this, he breathed on them, and said to them, 'Receive the Holy Spirit. If you forgive the sins of any, they are forgiven; if you retain the sins of any, they are retained.'" (Jn 20:19–23).

"'Christ is alive.' This is the great truth which fills our faith with meaning. Jesus, who died on the cross, has risen. He has triumphed over death; he has overcome sorrow, anguish and the power of darkness. 'Do not be terrified' was how the angels greeted the women who came to the tomb. 'Do not be terrified. You are looking for Jesus of Nazareth, who was crucified. He has risen; he is not here.' 'This is the day which the Lord has made; let us rejoice and be glad in it.'

"Easter is a time of joy—a joy not confined to this period of the liturgical year, but to be found really and fully in the Christian's heart. For Christ is alive. He is not someone who has gone, someone who existed for a time and then passed on, leaving us a wonderful example and a great memory.

"No, Christ is alive. Jesus is the Emmanuel: God with us. His resurrection shows us that God does not abandon his own. He promised he would not: 'Can a woman forget her baby that is still unweaned, pity no longer the son she bore in her womb? Even these may forget, yet I will not forget you.' And he has kept his promise. His delight is still to be with the sons of men.

"Christ is alive in his Church. 'I tell you the truth: it is to your advantage that I go away, for if I do not go away, the Counselor will not come to you; but if I go, I will send him to you.' That was what God planned: Jesus, dying on the cross, gave us the Spirit of truth and life. Christ stays in his Church, its sacraments, its liturgy, its preaching—in all that it does.

"In a special way Christ stays with us in the daily

offering of the holy Eucharist. That is why the Mass is the center and source of Christian life. In each and every Mass the complete Christ, head and body, is present. *Per Ipsum et cum Ipso et in Ipso.* ('Through Him and with Him and in Him.') For Christ is the way; he is the mediator; in him we find everything. Outside of him our life is empty. In Jesus Christ, and taught by him, 'we dare to say: Our Father.' We dare to call the Lord of heaven and earth our Father. The presence of the living Christ in the host is the guarantee, the source and the culmination of his presence in the world.

"Christ is alive in Christians. Our faith teaches us that man, in the state of grace, is divinized—filled with God. We are men and women, not angels. We are flesh and blood, people with sentiments and passions, with sorrows and joys. And this divinization affects everything human; it is a sort of foretaste of the final resurrection. 'Christ has risen from the dead, the first-fruits of those who have fallen asleep. For since by a man came death, by a man also comes resurrection of the dead. For as in Adam all die, so in Christ all will be made to live.'

"Christ's life is our life, just as he promised his apostles at the last supper: 'If anyone loves me, he will keep my word, and my Father will love him, and we will come to him and make our home with him.' That is why a Christian should live as Christ lived, making the affections of Christ his own, so that he can exclaim with St Paul: 'It is now no longer I that live, but Christ lives in me.'[47]

The Resurrection,
*Piero della Francesca
(1410/20–2492),
Sansepolcro,
Town Museum.*

---

[47] *Christ Is Passing By,* 102–103.

THE ASCENSION

"Now the eleven disciples went to Galilee, to the mountain to which Jesus had directed them. And when they saw him they worshipped him; but some doubted. And Jesus came and said to them, 'All authority in heaven and on earth has been given to me. Go therefore and make disciples of all nations, baptizing them in the name of the Father and of the Son and of the Holy Spirit, teaching them to observe all that I have commanded you; and Lo, I am with you always, to the close of the age'" (Mt 28:16–20).

"'But you shall receive power when the Holy Spirit has come upon you; and you shall be my witnesses in Jerusalem and in all Judea and Samaria and to the end of the earth.' And when he had said this, as they were looking on, he was lifted up, and a cloud took him out of their sight" (Acts 1:8–9).

The Ascension,
Rembrandt
(1606–1669).
Munich, Bavarian
Museum.

"Christ has gone up to heaven, but he has given to all honest human things a specific capacity to be redeemed. . . . And so I keep on repeating to you that the world can be made holy. We Christians have a special role to play in sanctifying it. We are to cleanse it from the occasions of sin with which we human beings have soiled it. We are to offer it to our Lord as a spiritual offering, presented to him and made acceptable through his grace and with our efforts. Strictly speaking, we cannot say that there is any noble human reality that does not have a supernatural dimension, for the divine Word has taken on a complete human nature and consecrated the world with his presence and with the work of his hands. The great mission that we have received in baptism is to redeem the world with Christ. . . .

". . . A great task awaits us. We cannot remain inactive, because our Lord has told us clearly, 'Trade till I come.' As long as we are awaiting the Lord's return, when he will come to take full possession of his kingdom, we cannot afford to relax. Spreading the kingdom of God isn't only an official task of those members of the Church who represent Christ because they have received sacred powers from him. 'You are also the body of Christ,' says the Apostle, with a specific command to fulfill. (1 *Cor* 12:27)

"There is so much to be done. Is it because in twenty centuries nothing has been done? In these two thousand years much work has been done. I don't think it would be fair or objective to discount, as some people want to do, the accomplishments of those who have gone before us. In two thousand years a great task has been accomplished, and it has often been accomplished very well. On other occasions there have been mistakes, making the Church lose ground, just as today there is loss of ground, fear and a timid attitude on the part of some, and at the same time no lack of courage and generosity in others. But, whatever the situation, the human race is being continually renewed. In each generation it is necessary to go on with the effort to help men realize the greatness of their vocation as children of God, to teach them to carry out the commandment of love for God and neighbor."[48]

"I never talk politics. I do not approve of committed Christians in the world forming a political-religious movement. That would be madness, even if it were motivated by a desire to spread the spirit of Christ in all the activities of men. What we have to do is put God in the heart of every single person, no matter who he is. Let us try to speak then in such a way that every Christian is able to bear witness to the faith he professes by example and word in his own circumstances, which are determined alike by his place in the Church and in civil life, as well as by ongoing events.

"By the very fact of being human, a Christian has a full right to live in the world. If he lets Christ live and reign in his heart, he will feel—quite noticeably—the saving effectiveness of our Lord in everything he does. It does not matter what his occupation is, whether his social status is 'high' or 'low'; for what appears to us to be an important achievement can be very low in God's sight; and what we call low or modest can in Christian terms be a summit of holiness and service."[49]

[48] *Christ Is Passing By,* 120–121.
[49] *Christ Is Passing By,* 183.

THE DESCENT OF THE HOLY SPIRIT

"When the day of Pentecost had come, they were all together in one place. And suddenly a sound came from heaven like the rush of a mighty wind, and it filled all the house where they were sitting. And there appeared to them tongues as of fire, distributed and resting on each one of them. And they were all filled with the Holy Spirit and began to speak in other tongues, as the Spirit gave them utterance.

"Now there were dwelling in Jerusalem Jews, devout men from every nation under heaven. And at this sound the multitude came together, and they were bewildered, because each one heard them speaking in his own language.

"But Peter, standing with the eleven, lifted up his voice and addressed them, 'Men of Judea. . . .'

"So those who received his word were baptized, and there were added that day about three thousand souls" (Acts 2:1–4).

Pentecost,
*Taddeo de
Bartolo
(1363–1422).
Perugia,
National Gallery.*

"The solemn coming of the Holy Spirit on Pentecost was not an isolated event. There is hardly a page in the Acts of the Apostles where we fail to read about him and the action by which he guides, directs and enlivens the life and work of the early Christian community. It is he who inspires the preaching of Saint Peter, who strengthens the faith of the disciples, who confirms with his presence the calling of the gentiles, who sends Saul and Barnabas to the distant lands where they will open new paths for the teaching of Jesus. In a word, his presence and doctrine are everywhere.

"The profound reality which we see in the texts of Holy Scripture is not a remembrance from the past, from some golden age of the Church which has since been buried in history. Despite the weaknesses and the sins of every one of us, it is the reality of today's Church and the Church of all time. 'I will ask the Father,' our Lord told his disciples, 'and he will give you another Counselor to dwell with you forever' (*Jn* 14:16). Jesus has kept his promise. He has risen from the dead, and in union with the eternal Father, he sends us the Holy Spirit to sanctify us and to give us life."[50]

"To live according to the Holy Spirit means to live by faith and hope and charity—to allow God to take possession of our lives and to change our hearts, to make us resemble him more and more. A mature and profound Christian life cannot be improvised, because it is the result of the growth of God's grace in us. In the Acts of the Apostles we find the early Christian community described in a single sentence, brief but full of meaning: 'and they continued steadfastly in the teaching of the apostles and in the communion of the breaking of the bread and in prayers.'

"...There are no second-class Christians, obliged to practice only a 'simplified version' of the Gospel. We have all received the same baptism, and although there is a great variety of spiritual gifts and human situations, there is only one Spirit who distributes God's gifts, only one faith, only one hope, only one love.

"And so we can apply to ourselves the question asked by the Apostle: 'Do you not know that you are the temple of God, and that the Spirit of God dwells in you?' (1 *Cor* 3:16) And we can understand it as an invitation to deal with God in a more personal and direct manner. For some, unfortunately, the Paraclete is the Great Stranger, the Great Unknown. He is merely a name that is mentioned, but not Someone, not one of the three Persons in the one God, with whom we can talk and with whose life we can live.

"We have to deal with him simply and trustingly, as we are taught by the Church in its liturgy. Then we will come to know our Lord better, and at the same time, we will realize more fully the great favor that has been granted us when we became Christians. We will see all the greatness and truth of the *divinization* to which I referred before, which is a sharing in God's own life."[51]

[50] *Christ Is Passing By,* 127–128.
[51] *Christ Is Passing By,* 134.

WORKS

Works

Saint Josemaría wrote prolifically over the course of his life. He would joke about the sound of his name: "My name is *Escrivá* and *escribo* [I write]. During his life, he published relatively little: he did not wish to create celebrity status for himself. Still, the books published during his lifetime or immediately after his death have seen numerous reprintings and translations, bringing to thousands upon thousands the light and warmth of the Christian faith, just as their author wished.

Despite this wide distribution, the quantity of his writings already published is smaller than that which still remains unpublished and will see the light of day in the future. This material is composed in large part of numerous spiritual writings and letters of a formative, theological, and pastoral character addressed to the men and women of Opus Dei from the decade of the 1930's until his death in 1975. In these writings, Saint Josemaría reveals himself as a pastor of souls who attentively guides the Christian formation of his sons and daughters.

Another portion of his unpublished writings are the personal notes he jotted down regarding his own spiritual life, an overflow of his spiritual intimacy with God. There also exist a large number of homilies and an ample correspondence with hundreds of people.

A brief description of his works presently available follows.

THE WAY

"Read these counsels slowly. Pause to meditate on these thoughts. They are things that I whisper in your ear—confiding them—as a friend, as a brother, as a father. And they are being heard by God." With these words, the best known and most popular of Saint Josemaria's books, *The Way,* begins.

This 1939 spiritual classic was his first book, being essentially a reworking of the smaller *Consideraciones Espirituales* published a few years earlier. The 999 points (the number deliberately chosen as a multiple of 3 out of devotion to the Trinity) cover aspects of Christian life needed in order to really be and to act like a child of God in the middle of the world: starting from personal character and ending with the apostolate, passing through prayer, work, and virtue. The purpose is laid out in the prologue: "I will only stir your memory, so that some thought will arise and strike you; and so you will better your life and set out along ways of prayer and of Love. And in the end you will be a more worthy soul."

"I wrote most of the book," said the author, in an interview with *Le Figaro* in 1966, "in 1934, summarizing my priestly experience for the benefit of all the souls with whom I was in contact, whether they were in Opus Dei or not . . . It is not a book solely for members of Opus Dei. It is for everyone, whether Christian or non-Christian. *The Way* must be read with a minimum of supernatural spirit, interior life, and apostolic feeling. It is not a code for the man of action. The book's aim is to help people to become God's friends, to love him, and to serve all men and women."

The Way has sold 4.5 million copies and has been translated into 44 languages.

FURROW

In a note to a 1950 edition of *The Way,* Saint Josemaría promised readers a new book—*Furrow*—soon to be published. The material was written and organized into chapter headings; only the numbering of the points of meditation and a stylistic revision remained. However, it would not be until 1986 that the work was published posthumously, due to his intense work founding and governing Opus Dei, his pastoral work and his other tasks in the service of the Church.

Just like *The Way,* it is the fruit of Saint Josemaría's spiritual life and experience with souls. It consists of 1000 brief points to work the ground, to plow furrows, in preparation for the soul's reception of the seeds of the Word. This was an idea dear to Saint Josemaría: "My reader and friend, let me help your soul contemplate the human virtues, for grace works upon nature." The infused virtues find support in natural virtues; human qualities are indispensable to work for the good on the supernatural plane.

As Álvaro del Portillo writes in the foreword, "Monsignor Escriva's teaching brings together the human and the divine aspects of Christian perfection. That must be so when the Catholic doctrine on the Incarnate Word is known in depth and when it is loved, and lived, passionately. The practical and vital consequences of that joyful reality are clearly drawn in *Furrow.*"

To date, 500,000 copies have been sold in 19 languages.

THE FORGE

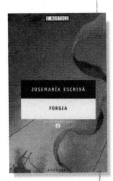

This book, a compilation of spiritual annotations of Josemaría Escrivá appearing in 1987, completes the trilogy aimed at facilitating personal prayer that began with *The Way* and continued with *Furrow*. Similar in structure to these two, it consists of 1055 points organized in 13 chapters centered on the soul's journey toward identification with Christ. The author's prologue captures its purpose nicely:

> There was a mother,
> who, like all mothers,
> was passionately fond of her little child,
> whom she called
> her prince, her king,
> her treasure, her very sun.
>
> I thought of you.
>
> And I understood
> —for what father does not carry
> deep inside some maternal feelings?—
> that it was no exaggeration
> for that good mother to say:
>
> you are more than a treasure,
> you are worth more than the sun itself:
> you are worth all Christ's Blood!
>
> How can I fail to take up your soul
> —pure gold—
> and place it in *the forge,*
> and fashion it with fire and hammer,
> until that gold nugget is turned
> into a splendid jewel
> to be offered to my God,
> to your God?

The Forge has been translated into 14 languages and has sold over 400,000 copies.

HOLY ROSARY

One December morning in 1931, Fr. Josemaría dashed off this small book in one sitting, just after celebrating Mass. He poured into these pages an example of his way of meditating the mysteries of the life of Jesus and Mary, and of reciting the Rosary.

At that time the young founder was going from one side of Madrid to the other on pastoral visits, wrapped in his cloak, fingering the beads of his Rosary, immersed in a contemplative praying of the fifteen mysteries of the Rosary. It was the prayer of a child who abandoned himself into the arms of his mother precisely because he had need of much strength.

Contemplation and spiritual childhood: these are the two solid pillars of the text. "I must tell them a secret," the author commences, "which may very well be the beginning of the road that Christ wants them to follow. My friend, if you want to be great, become little. To be little you have to believe as children believe, to love as children love, to abandon yourself as children do . . . to pray as children pray. You have to do all this if you are going to achieve what I am going to tell you in these lines: *The beginning of the way,* at the end of which you will find yourself completely carried away by love for Jesus, is a trusting love for Mary."

Contemplation: to participate in the mystery from within, as one more character present. "We will admire his thirty years of hidden life . . . We will be present at his Passion and death . . . We will be awed by the glory of his Resurrection . . ." This is a Rosary solidly anchored in Scripture.

Striking is the literary, at times poetic, quality of the text. Parting with his reader, he confides, "My friend: I have told you just part of my secret. It is up to you, with God's help, to discover the rest. Take courage. Be faithful. Become little. Our Lord hides from the proud and reveals the treasures of his grace to the humble. Don't worry if, when thinking on your own, daring and childish words and affections arise in your heart. This is what Jesus wants, and Mary is encouraging you. If you say the Rosary in this way, you will learn to pray well."

Over 700,000 copies have been sold in 23 languages.

THE WAY OF THE CROSS

"My Lord and my God, under the loving eyes of our Mother, we are making ready to accompany you along this path of sorrow, which was the price for our redemption. We wish to suffer all that you suffered, to offer you our poor, contrite hearts, because you are innocent, and yet you are going to die for us, who are the only really guilty ones. My Mother, Virgin of sorrows, help me to relive those bitter hours which your Son wished to spend on earth, so that we, who were made from a handful of clay, may finally live *in libertatem gloriae filiorum Dei,* in the freedom and glory of the children of God."

This introductory prayer composed by Saint Josemaría summarizes the book's raison d'être: *The Way of the Cross,* just like *Holy Rosary* is a book for contemplation. The reader accompanies Christ through the fourteen traditional stations, gazing in wonder and contrition at the redemptive love in the sufferings of Christ. After the description of each station, several points for meditation are mentioned.

Álvaro del Portillo comments in the foreword that when Saint Josemaría encouraged Christians to follow, in the footsteps of Jesus, the way of the Cross by *placing themselves* in the wounds of Christ crucified, "he was doing no more than pass on his own experience, pointing out the short cut he had been using throughout his life, and which led him to the highest peaks of spiritual life. His love for Jesus was always something real, tangible and strong; it was tender, filial and very moving."

Published posthumously in 1981, it has sold 500,000 copies in 19 languages.

CHRIST IS PASSING BY

In 1973, Saint Josemaría prepared this book, drawing on his abundant preaching. It consists of 18 sermons preached between 1951 and 1971 that follow the feasts of the liturgical year, from Advent to the Solemnity of Christ the King.

Word and life. The text is notable for its simple entry into the heart of Christian truth. Scripture inspires every page, not as erudition, but as a way of life.

While not constituting a theological treatise properly speaking, it nonetheless delves deeply into the truth that saves, rendering it accessible to everyone. If one were to pick out a connecting thread between the texts, it would have to be that of divine filiation, the marvelous reality that can guide the life of the Christian passing through the middle of the world: I am a child of God.

The great topics of Christianity run through these pages: the Christian vocation, the example of Jesus Christ, marriage as a divine calling, work as a way of sanctification and apostolate, the freedom of the children of God, the ascetical struggle, the Eucharist, the Holy Spirit, the Blessed Mother . . . Not only at the beginning of the first homily, but also at each juncture one discerns the gentle voice of a saint that encourages as he preaches: "'Make me to know your ways, O Lord, teach me your paths.' (*Ps* 24:4) We ask the Lord to guide us, to show us his footprints, so we can set out to attain the fullness of his commandments, which is charity."

Over 500,000 copies in 14 languages have been sold.

FRIENDS OF GOD

A canticle to ordinary life, addressed to ordinary Christians, about the extraordinary surprise God has in store for them. This compilation was the first posthumous work of Saint Josemaría. Issued in 1977, its 18 homilies preached between 1941 and 1968 touch on the great subjects of Christian spirituality according to the foundational inspiration of Saint Josemaría: the greatness of ordinary life, the gift of freedom, the importance of natural virtues, humility, detachment, chastity, prayer, faith, hope, charity, apostolate . . .

His clear, concise, gracious language speaks to ordinary Christians. And precisely to them he offers the high goal of contemplation, with the conviction that everyone can and should strive for holiness without qualifications: "In recommending this unbroken union with God am I not presenting an ideal so sublime that it is unattainable by the majority of Christians? Certainly the goal is high but it is not unattainable."

"The path that leads to holiness is the path of prayer: and prayer takes root and grows in the soul little by little, like the tiny seed which later develops into a tree with many branches.

"First one brief aspiration, then another, and another . . . till our fervor seems insufficient, because words are too poor . . .: then this gives way to intimacy with God, looking at God without needing rest or feeling tired. We begin to live as captives, as prisoners. And while we carry out as perfectly as we can (with all our mistakes and limitations) the tasks allotted to us by our situation and duties, our soul longs to escape. It is drawn towards God like iron drawn by a magnet. One begins to love Jesus, in a more effective way, with the sweet and gentle surprise of his encounter."

What basis, what grounds do Christians have, for nurturing such amazing aspirations in their lives? Álvaro del Portillo notes in the foreword, "The answer comes as a sort of refrain, again and again, right through these homilies: it is the humble sense of daring 'of the person who, knowing himself to be poor and weak, knows also that he is a son of God.'"

Over 400,000 copies in 13 languages have been sold.

IN LOVE WITH THE CHURCH

The core of this book is three homilies on themes related to the Church, given in 1972–73, when the author suffered much over the confusion of the post-conciliar years. The title captures his attitude of filial love for the Spouse of Christ that permeates these pages.

The first homily, *Loyalty to the Church,* reflects on the marks of the Church (one, holy, catholic, apostolic). The second, The *Supernatural Aim of the Church,* pays homage to the Church as the 'universal sacrament of salvation,' and rejects the attempts to limit the Church to a purely human goal.

A Priest Forever, the third homily, ponders the nature of the Catholic priesthood, its necessity, dignity, relation to the Mass, as well as the relation between priests and laity in the Church.

These three homilies were published separately before his death. In 1985 they were collected into the Spanish *Amar a la Iglesia.* Two subsequent English translations were published under two different titles, *In Love with the Church* and *In God's Household.* Both English translations added an improved translation of the homily *Passionately Loving the World* from the book *Conversations with Monsignor Escrivá,* as well as an epilogue by Álvaro del Portillo written on the 10th anniversary of Saint Josemaría's death.

CONVERSATIONS WITH JOSEMARÍA ESCRIVÁ

In the years immediately after Vatican II, Saint Josemaría granted interviews to various newspapers and magazines around the world, such as *Time, Le Figaro,* and *The New York Times.* In them the founder broached a number of topics, including the mission of the university, the role of women in the Church and in society, and the nature and apostolates of Opus Dei.

Seven of these interviews, which reflect his supernatural sense, his cordiality, his love of freedom in defending ideals and in reaching out in dialogue, are collected in this volume, published in 1968. These are joined by the text of a famous homily, *Passionately Loving the World,* given by the founder on the campus of the University of Navarre in 1967.

Over 300,000 copies in 9 languages have been sold.

Chronology

1902—January 9. Josemaría Escrivá is born in Barbastro. January 13. He is baptized in the parish church of our Lady of the Assumption, in Barbastro.

1904—He falls gravely ill and is suddenly cured through the intercession of our Lady of Torreciudad.

1912—April 23. He receives his First Holy Communion.

1915—His father's business fails, and the whole family moves to Logrono.

1917—He has inklings of his vocation. The last days of 1917, or the first of 1918, footprints in the snow of the bare feet of a Carmelite stir up in him an intense desire to love God. He decides to become a priest.

1918—He begins his ecclesiastical studies as a day student at the seminary of Logroño.

1920—He moves to Saragossa to finish his priestly studies at the pontifical university of the archdiocese. He lives at the seminary of St. Francis de Paula.

1923—He begins to study for a Licentiate degree in Law at the University of Saragossa.

1925—March 28. He receives priestly ordination in the church of the Seminary of St. Charles. He celebrates his first Mass in the Basilica of our Lady of the Pillar, on March 30, praying for the repose of his father. The next day he is assigned to substitute the parish priest in Perdiguera, outside Saragossa.

1927—In January he receives his Licentiate in Law, and on April 19 he moves to Madrid to study towards a doctorate in Civil Law.

1928—October 2. By divine inspiration, he founds Opus Dei in Madrid—a way of sanctification through professional work and in the fulfillment of one's ordinary duties.

1930—February 14. While he celebrates Mass in Madrid, God makes him understand that Opus Dei is also intended for women.

1933—He opens the first center of Opus Dei, the DYA Academy, for students.

1934—He publishes in Cuenca *Consideraciones Espirituales*, which is a predecessor of *The Way*.

1936—The Spanish Civil War. Religious persecution breaks out. Josemaría Escrivá has to seek refuge in various places. Plans to bring Opus Dei to other countries are put on hold.

1937—The founder crosses the Pyrenees to Andorra on his way to the part of Spain from which he can restart the apostolate of the Work.

1939—He publishes in Valencia the first edition of *The Way*.

1941—March 19. The bishop of Madrid, Leopoldo Eijo y Garay, grants the first diocesan approval of Opus Dei.

1943—February 14. During Mass our Lord makes him see the resolution of a canonical problem. Henceforth, some faithful of Opus Dei can be ordained priests; and thus is born the Priestly Society of the Holy Cross.

1944—June 25. First priestly ordination of faithful of Opus Dei, administered by the bishop of Madrid.

1946—The founder of Opus Dei moves to Rome.

1947—February 24. The Holy See grants the first pontifical approval.

1948—June 29. He establishes in Rome the Roman College of the Holy Cross, for the formation of men of Opus Dei who come from all over the world.

1950—June 16. Pope Pius XII grants definitive approval to Opus Dei. Secular priests can belong to the Priestly Society of the Holy Cross. It also becomes possible to name non-Catholics and even non-Christians as cooperators of Opus Dei.

1953—December 12. He establishes the Roman College of Holy Mary, an international center for the spiritual, theological and apostolic formation of women in Opus Dei.

1957—He is named member of the Pontifical Academy of Theology and Consultor of the Congregation of Seminaries.

1960—October 21. He receives an honorary doctorate from the University of Saragossa. October 25. He erects the University of Navarre.

1961—Pope John XXIII names him Consultor of the Pontificial Commission for the Authentic Interpretation of the Code of Canon Law.

1962—October 11. Vatican II begins. The founder of Opus Dei asks all his children in Opus Dei for prayers for the supernatural effectiveness of the Council.

1965—November 21. Pope Paul VI inaugurates Centro ELIS for the professional training of manual workers.

1967—Publication of *Conversations with Msgr. Josemaría Escrivá*.

1969—Extraordinary General Congress of Opus Dei in Rome to study its transformation into a personal prelature, a canonical entity foreseen by Vatican II which corresponded to the pastoral phenomenon of the Work.

1970—He travels to Mexico to pray at the Shrine of our Lady of Guadalupe.

1972—Josemaría Escrivá travels for two months through Spain and Portugal and meets with thousands of people.

1973—In March, *Christ Is Passing By* is published. Another volume of homilies, *Friends of God*, will be published—like *Furrow, The Forge*, and *Way of the Cross*—after his death.

1974—He travels to six countries of South America, Brazil, Argentina, Chile, Peru, Ecuador and Venezuela, where he carries out a wide work of catechesis among his children and many other persons.

1975—Last pastoral visit of Josemaría Escrivá to America, Venezuela and Guatemala. May 25. He visits Barbastro and Torreciudad. June 26. Josemaría Escrivá dies in Rome. At that time, there were 60,000 persons belonging to Opus Dei. July 7. Inauguration of the Shrine of our Lady of Torreciudad, near Barbastro, his birthplace. September 15. Alvaro del Portillo is elected to succeed the founder of Opus Dei.

1981—May 12. The cause of canonization of Msgr. Josemaría Escrivá opens in Rome.

1982—November 28. Pope John Paul II erects Opus Dei as a personal prelature, a legal framework anticipated by the founder, and names Msgr. Alvaro del Portillo as prelate.

1990—April 9. Publication of the Decree on Heroic Virtue of the Venerable Servant of God Josemaría Escrivá.

1991—July 6. Publication of the Decree on a miraculous cure attributed to his intercession.

1992—May 17. Pope John Paul II beatifies Josemaría Escrivá in St. Peter's Square in Rome.

2001—December 20. Publication of the Decree on a second miraculous cure attributed to his intercession.

2002—October 6. Canonization of Josemaría Escrivá.